Gibraltar

Travel guide 2025

Your ultimate journey through history, culture, and breathtaking landscapes.

David E. Welter

1

INTRODUCTION

I arrived on a crisp morning, the air infused with the salty aroma of the sea. My first glance at the Rock of Gibraltar was breathtaking. Standing magnificently, it appeared to watch over the city below with a timeless stare. This limestone monolith is more than simply a natural wonder; it is Gibraltar's throbbing heart, full of centuries of history.

My expedition began in the Great Siege Tunnels, a complex network of corridors carved out of solid rock by British soldiers in the 18th century. As I strolled down the dimly lighted tunnels, I could almost hear the sounds of the past—soldiers' boots clattering on stone, the distant thunder of guns. The strategic importance of this castle was evident, and I couldn't help but respect the creativity and dedication of those who hand-carved these tunnels.

As I emerged from the tunnels, I found myself in St. Michael's Cave, a breathtaking natural grotto that has served many roles throughout the millennia. With its stunning stalactites and stalagmites, it was like entering another universe. The cave's acoustics are just wonderful, making it a favorite music location. I sat for a time, absorbing the cave's natural beauty and peace, feeling a strong connection to the land.

No visit to Gibraltar is complete without seeing its most renowned residents, the Barbary macaques. These cheeky monkeys travel freely throughout the Upper Rock Nature Reserve, and they are just as interested in us as we are in them. I had a close encounter with a very brave macaque who appeared to be searching my rucksack for goodies. It served as a fun reminder of the delicate balance that exists between animals and human activities in this particular ecosystem.

The Moorish Castle was next on my itinerary, a tribute to Gibraltar's rich and diverse past. Built in the eighth century, this castle has seen several fights and changes of authority. Standing atop its medieval walls, I took in the panoramic views of the Mediterranean Sea and the far coastlines of Africa. The sense of history was tremendous, and I could almost see the Moors defending their fortress against invaders.

Exploring the town center felt like walking into a rich patchwork of cultures. Main Street was bustling with activity, surrounded by attractive stores, cozy cafes, and vibrant markets. The architecture, food, and even the talk of inhabitants and tourists all reflected a combination of British and Mediterranean influences. I engaged in some retail therapy, purchasing unusual gifts and sampling delectable local foods such as Valentina, a chickpea flour pancake that is a hallmark of Gibraltarian cuisine.

One of the pleasures of my vacation was a visit to Catalan Bay, a lovely fishing community on the Rock's eastern side. The colorful homes, golden sand, and calm waves produced a postcard-worthy image. I spent a quiet afternoon lounging in the sun, watching fisherman fix their nets and listening to the calming sounds of the water. It was the ideal vacation from the rush and bustle of everyday life.

As the sun began to drop, I headed to Europa Point, Gibraltar's southernmost point. The tall Europa Point Lighthouse serves as a sentinel, directing ships across the dangerous seas of the Strait of Gibraltar. The vistas were truly breathtaking—on a clear day, you could see as far as Morocco's coast. I stood there, mesmerized by the play of light on the lake, pondering on the innumerable sailors who had passed through these waters throughout the years.

However, Gibraltar is much more than simply history and natural beauty. It's also a sanctuary for outdoor lovers. I joined a group of other explorers for a day of rock climbing on the cliffs of The Rock. The exhilaration of climbing these old cliffs with the sea reaching out below was wonderful. My guide, a seasoned climber, regaled us with anecdotes about the difficulties and rewards of climbing in such a unique environment.

To change things up, I went on a calm dolphin-watching cruise in the Bay of Gibraltar. The area is home to various kinds of dolphins, and it wasn't long before we noticed a joyful pod leaping and playing in the surf. Watching these beautiful creatures in their native home served as a humble reminder of the natural world's beauty and magnificence.

Gibraltar's nightlife is another part of its appeal. I spent the evening at Casemates Square, the city's social hub. The area comes alive at night, with live music, street performers, and a lively atmosphere. I had a lovely evening at a local restaurant, savoring fresh fish and classic British cuisine. We had a terrific day with the friendly locals and fellow travelers, exchanging tales and travel ideas till late at night.

My last day in Gibraltar was a bittersweet goodbye. I went to the Gibraltar Museum, which provides an interesting view into the region's history, from ancient times to the present. The museum's displays, which included the remains of a

Neanderthal infant unearthed in Gibraltar, emphasized the area's rich and diverse past.

As I boarded my trip home, I felt overwhelmed with appreciation for the memories and experiences I had accumulated in Gibraltar. This little area, with its rich history, breathtaking scenery, and kind people, had made an unforgettable impression on my spirit. I knew that one day I'd return to this magical corner of the earth, eager to discover more of its hidden gems.

The Unique Identity of Gibraltar

Gibraltar. It's more than just a dot on a map; it's a bustling hub of life and history, an interesting confluence of cultures, and a lasting emblem of perseverance.

When you first arrive in Gibraltar, the Rock meets you with a commanding presence. This limestone promontory is more than simply a geographical marker; it represents the very essence of the region. As you walk through its streets, you'll discover an intriguing mix of British charm with Mediterranean flare. Red telephone booths stand out against a backdrop of sun-drenched plazas where both residents and visitors enjoy their morning coffee.

Gibraltar's past is at the core of its identity. This little peninsula has witnessed everything, from the ancient Phoenicians to the British Empire. Each age left its imprint, creating a complex tapestry of influences. The Moorish Castle commemorates the medieval period, while the Great Siege Tunnels depict 18th-century strategic military strength.

Walking through the town center, you're immersed in a bustling environment. Main Street is bustling with activity, with everything from British high street names to charming local stores selling unique items. The inhabitants of Gibraltar are as diverse as the things on show, speaking a mix of English, Spanish, and Llanito, a unique native dialect. It's a mixing pot of customs and tales, and every street corner has a story to tell.

But Gibraltar is more than simply its history; it is also a forward-thinking place with a vibrant culture. The calendar is full of festivals and activities that celebrate this enclave's distinct personality all year. From the National Day celebrations, which transform the town into a sea of red and white, to the Calentita Food Festival, which displays the finest of Gibraltarian food, there's always something to do.

Gibraltar's natural splendor adds another chapter to its story. The Mediterranean environment provides warm winters and pleasant summers, ideal for outdoor excursions. The Upper Rock Nature Reserve provides stunning panoramic vistas. You may also see the famed Barbary macaques, Europe's sole wild monkey population, which adds to the wilderness feel of your stay.

In Gibraltar, every moment is infused with a distinct combination of old and new. It's a site where history is alive in the present, cultures collide, and each visitor becomes a part of the continuing drama. This is more than simply a vacation spot; it's a live, breathing story that begs you to become a character within its pages.

Historical Background

Gibraltar's history is a narrative of strategic importance, cultural interaction, and endurance. This little peninsula has been desired by several nations over the years, each leaving a unique stamp on the region.

Gibraltar's first known residents were the Neanderthals, who lived in the Rock's caves about 50,000 years ago. Their existence is proved by fossils and implements discovered in locations such as Gorham's Cave, which give insight into the life of these ancient people.

Fast forward to the eighth century, when the Moors, commanded by Tariq ibn Ziyad, crossed the Strait of Gibraltar to claim the Rock. Gibraltar's name is taken from his name, Jabal Tariq, or "Mountain of Tariq." The Moors constructed several fortresses, notably the renowned Moorish Castle, which survives today as a tribute to their architectural brilliance and strategic vision.

In 1462, the Spanish regained Gibraltar from the Moors, ushering in a lengthy period of Spanish dominance. The Rock's strategic location at the Mediterranean's entry made it a valuable asset, which resulted in repeated confrontations and power struggles.

The War of the Spanish Succession in the early 18th century saw Gibraltar change hands once more. An Anglo-Dutch force took Gibraltar in 1704, and the Treaty of Utrecht, signed in 1713, legally handed the peninsula to Britain. This signaled the start of Gibraltar's metamorphosis into an important British naval base.

Throughout the 18th and 19th centuries, Gibraltar's military importance increased. The Great Siege of Gibraltar (1779-

1783) was a watershed moment in this time. Spanish and French armies besieged the Rock, attempting to recapture it from the British. Despite overwhelming odds, the British defenders stood fast, and the siege eventually failed. The enormous network of tunnels cut into the Rock at this time demonstrates the defenders' resourcefulness and determination.

Gibraltar's status as a strategic naval base lasted into the twentieth century. During World War II, the Rock was a crucial bastion for the Allies. Its defenses were progressively strengthened, and many of the wartime bunkers and tunnels are still accessible today, providing insight into Gibraltar's strategic importance throughout the struggle.

Gibraltar had additional obstacles in defining its identity after the conflict. The connection with Spain remained difficult, ending in the Spanish government closing the border in 1969. This time of seclusion instilled a strong feeling of community and self-reliance in Gibraltarians. The border was entirely reopened in 1985, ushering in a new age of collaboration and development.

Today, Gibraltar is a lively melting pot of cultures, reflecting its varied past. British, Spanish, and Moorish influences may be seen in the architecture, food, and daily life. The Rock is a symbol of tenacity, having endured centuries of strife and upheaval. Its rich past is maintained not just in museums and historical places, but also in the people's tales and traditions.

Geography and Climate

Gibraltar is a remarkable area, both physically confined and wonderfully diversified. This British Overseas Territory, which covers only 6.7 square kilometers, is a patchwork of natural beauties and urban charm.

Without question, the Rock of Gibraltar is Gibraltar's most spectacular landmark. This massive limestone promontory rises to 426 meters and dominates the landscape. It is a natural stronghold that has had a profound impact on the territory's history and defense. The Rock is more than simply a monolith; it's full of caverns and tunnels, each with its narrative. Among these, St. Michael's Cave stands out as a spectacular natural grotto that has been utilized for a variety of reasons over the centuries.

Beyond the Rock, Gibraltar's land descends gently down to the sea, resulting in a diversity of coastal settings. To the east, you'll discover the sandy beaches of Eastern Beach and Catalan Bay, which are ideal for relaxing and swimming. The western side is home to the port and marinas, such as Queensway Quay

Marina and Ocean Village, which are lively centers of activity and leisure.

Despite its modest size, Gibraltar has several microclimates. The Mediterranean climate has hot, dry summers and warm, rainy winters. Summers are often bright, with temperatures reaching as high as 30°C (86°F). It's the perfect time to visit the beach and participate in outdoor activities. Winters, on the other hand, are moderate, with temperatures seldom falling below 10°C (50°F) and periodic rains to maintain the landscape lush and bright.

Gibraltar's unique location at the gateway to the Mediterranean attracts a diverse range of animals. The Upper Rock Nature Reserve is home to the famed Barbary macaques, Europe's sole wild monkey population. These attractive primates are a popular attraction, frequently seen playing or foraging near the Apes' Den.

Birdwatchers are also in for a treat. Gibraltar is located along a major migratory path, giving it an excellent place to observe a variety of bird species, particularly during the spring and fall migrations. The skies above the Rock come alive with flocks of birds on their trip between Europe and Africa.

Gibraltar's strategic position also results in a thriving marine ecosystem. Dolphins of several species live in the seas surrounding the Rock and are regularly seen playing in the Bay of Gibraltar. Dolphin-watching cruises are popular, providing an opportunity to see these wonderful creatures up close.

Gibraltar's temperature and location make it an ideal year-round getaway. Whether you're climbing the Rock, discovering its historic tunnels, relaxing on its beaches, or simply admiring the breathtaking vistas, there's always something to pique your interest in this extraordinary part of the globe.

Language and Culture

Gibraltar's cultural environment is as diverse as its past. Despite its tiny size, Gibraltar has a diverse range of languages, traditions, and influences, resulting in a distinct cultural identity.

The language of Gibraltar is a remarkable tapestry. English is the official language of government, education, and everyday business. However, many Gibraltarians are multilingual, speaking both English and Spanish. This bilingualism reflects the territory's geographical proximity to Spain, as well as its historical links. Walking around the streets of Gibraltar, you'll hear a seamless blend of English and Spanish, sometimes in the same discussion. This language duality reflects the people's flexibility and cosmopolitan character.

But Gibraltar's linguistic attractiveness does not end there. The people also speak Llanito, a distinct dialect that combines English, Spanish, and parts of other languages including Genoese and Hebrew. Llanito reflects Gibraltar's rich past and is spoken with a particular Gibraltarian flare. Mixing words like "¿Qué pasa?" ("What's happening?") with English sentences creates a vibrant and dynamic communication style.

Gibraltar's culture is a dynamic mix of Mediterranean and British influences. Festivals and public holidays are enthusiastically observed, reflecting the territory's multicultural culture. National Day, which takes place on September 10th, is one of the most major events. The whole community dresses in red and white, the colors of Gibraltar's flag, and congregates in Casemates Square for a day of festivities, music, and fireworks. It's a day of pride and communal spirit that celebrates Gibraltar's distinctive personality.

Another cultural highlight is the Calentita Food Festival, which takes place every year to showcase Gibraltar's gastronomic variety. The festival serves a diverse range of cuisine from several countries, reflecting the region's diversified palette.

From classic British fish and chips to Spanish tapas and Moroccan tagine, the festival offers a culinary voyage across the world. Calentita, a chickpea flour pancake, is a local specialty and must-try food that inspired the festival's name.

Religious festivals have an essential part in Gibraltarian culture. The area is home to a diverse range of religious communities, and significant religious festivals are observed by everybody, regardless of creed. The combination of Catholic, Jewish, Muslim, and Hindu traditions results in a complex tapestry of religious devotion. It is not uncommon to witness a Jewish celebration taking place next to a Catholic procession, demonstrating the peaceful coexistence of different religions.

Art and music are vital to Gibraltar's cultural life. Gibraltar has a strong arts sector, with local artists inspired by the territory's history, nature, and cosmopolitan atmosphere. Galleries like the Fine Arts Gallery exhibit works by both local and foreign artists, fostering cultural interchange and artistic expression.

Music is also significant, with events like the Gibraltar Music Festival attracting both worldwide and local musicians. The event, hosted at Victoria Stadium, celebrates music and community by bringing people together to see acts ranging from rock and pop to classical and flamenco.

Gibraltar's everyday life is a mix of relaxed Mediterranean pace and British orderliness. The café culture is prominent, with inhabitants taking lengthy, leisurely coffee breaks and meals at the various cafés and restaurants that line the streets. The cuisine reflects Gibraltar's mixed background, combining Mediterranean flavors with British comfort food. Given Gibraltar's seaside position, seafood is in high demand, and local favorites include Calentita and Vanessa (another chickpea-based specialty).

In essence, Gibraltar is a location where cultures come together and cohabit peacefully. The combination of languages, cultures, and influences results in a lively and active community. It's a town where church bells sound next to the call to prayer, English pubs coexist with Spanish tapas bars, and every street corner has a tale to tell. Gibraltar's distinct cultural character demonstrates the tenacity and flexibility of its people, making it an intriguing destination to visit and experience.

1 WEEK ITINERY

Day One: Arrival and Orientation
Morning: Arrive in Gibraltar and check into your accommodations.

Afternoon: Take a stroll along Main Street to get a sense of the area. Visit the Gibraltar Museum to learn about the territory's history.

Evening: Have a welcome supper at a local restaurant and taste traditional foods such as calentita and panissa.

Day 2: Rock of Gibraltar

Morning: Take the cable car to the summit of the Rock of Gibraltar for stunning views of the surrounding area.

Afternoon: Visit the Upper Rock Nature Reserve, including the Apes' Den, to observe the iconic Barbary macaques.

Evening: Take a guided tour of St. Michael's Cave, a beautiful natural grotto.

Day 3: Historic Sites

Morning: Explore the Great Siege Tunnels, a vast network of tunnels excavated during the Great Siege of Gibraltar.

Afternoon: Explore the Moorish Castle, one of Gibraltar's oldest structures, and learn about its medieval history.

Evening: Relax in a town center café and listen to some local music.

Day 4: Nature & Wildlife

Morning: Take a walk down the Mediterranean Steps, which offers panoramic views and the opportunity to see local animals.

Afternoon: Go on a dolphin-watching excursion in the Bay of Gibraltar to observe these lively creatures up close.

Evening: Dine at a beachfront restaurant and watch the sunset over the sea.

Day 5: Cultural immersion.

Morning: Take a guided tour of the Gibraltar Nature Reserve to learn about the area's plants and animals.

Afternoon: Visit local markets and stores to pick up gifts and learn about the rich local culture.

Evening: If possible, attend a cultural event or festival to learn about Gibraltar's customs.

Day 6: Relaxation and Leisure

Morning: Spend the morning at Catalan Bay, a lovely fishing hamlet with golden dunes and crystal blue seas.

Afternoon: Relax on the beach or enjoy a leisurely boat ride around the Rock.

Evening: Have a seafood meal at a local restaurant, savoring the fresh catch of the day.

Day 7: Farewell to Gibraltar
Morning: Visit Europa Point, Gibraltar's southernmost point, and enjoy the breathtaking views of the Strait of Gibraltar and Morocco's coastline.

Afternoon: Take a last trip down Main Street, possibly stopping at a few more stores or cafés.

Evening: Reflect on your trip and prepare to go.

Arriving in Gibraltar

Travel by Air

Traveling to Gibraltar by air is an adventure that begins far before you arrive. As your jet descends, you'll be treated to breathtaking views of the Rock of Gibraltar rising abruptly from the sea, setting the scene for your tour.

When you arrive at Gibraltar International Airport, you will see something pretty extraordinary: the runway connects with a major road. Winston Churchill Avenue, the major route into town, is blocked to traffic whenever a jet comes or departs, making it one of the few airports in the world with such an unusual configuration. It's a peculiarity that lends a special flavor to your arrival.

When you get off the plane, you are greeted by a warm Mediterranean wind, which contrasts sharply with the cabin air. The airport is tiny and efficient, reflecting Gibraltar's compact character. You won't have to spend much time in long queues here, so you may begin your journey practically immediately.

A short taxi trip from the airport will take you to the center of Gibraltar. Along the route, you'll pass past ancient landmarks and lively streets, giving you a sense of the diverse cultures that make this town so special. The trip provides views of the Rock, a continual and breathtaking backdrop to your adventure.

If you want a more picturesque route, consider walking from the airport to the town center. It's a pleasant 20-minute walk that allows you to take in the scenery and noises. Crossing the runway on foot is an unforgettable experience that offers a unique viewpoint on Gibraltar's fusion of daily life and aviation travel.

Your first experience of Gibraltar by flight will undoubtedly be unforgettable, regardless of how you arrive. The smooth transition from sky to street, together with the friendly mood, establishes the tone for the remainder of your visit. As you settle here, you'll see that this little yet active region is full of surprises waiting to be discovered around every turn.

Arriving by Sea

Arriving in Gibraltar by boat is an unforgettable experience that combines the thrill of travel with the timeless attraction of maritime adventure. As your ship approaches the peninsula, you'll notice the towering silhouette of the Rock of Gibraltar, which rises from the horizon like a sentinel. The vista of this prominent monument against the blue Mediterranean Sea is just magnificent.

Cruise ships and ferries often dock at Gibraltar Port, which is located on the western edge of the enclave. As your ship enters the harbor, you will be treated to panoramic views of the town's skyline, which combines British and Mediterranean architecture. The busy port, with its mix of fishing boats, yachts, and commercial vessels, is a hub of activity that reflects Gibraltar's robust marine culture.

Stepping off the ship, the sea wind conveys the fragrances of the ocean and the promise of adventure. The port area is well-organized, with convenient access to the rest of Gibraltar. Just a short walk from the pier, you'll be in the heart of town, ready to explore.

One of the first things to do when you arrive is take a stroll along the shore. Queensway Quay Marina and Ocean Village

Marina, both within walking distance of the port, provide an enjoyable introduction to Gibraltar's seaside appeal. You may admire the elegant yachts, have a coffee at one of the riverfront cafés, and drink up the easygoing ambiance.

Consider visiting the Gibraltar Marine Museum to learn more about the country's marine heritage. Located near the harbor, this museum offers unique insights into the region's nautical and shipping legacy, from ancient times to the present. The exhibits contain replicas of old ships, marine artifacts, and stories about the sailors who previously sailed these seas.

As you progress through the town, the sights, sounds, and flavors of Gibraltar become more apparent. The town center is a short walk away, with a mix of small alleyways, vibrant markets, and ancient sites. Main Street, with its stores, restaurants, and bars, creates a bustling and pleasant ambiance. It's the ideal site to begin your journey and gain a sense of the local culture.

One of the advantages of coming by boat is the chance to see Gibraltar's coastline from a different angle. Consider taking a boat cruise to view the Rock from the water. These trips frequently include stops at areas of interest, such as Europa Point, Gibraltar's southernmost point, where you can see the famous lighthouse and enjoy breathtaking views across the Strait of Gibraltar to the coast of Africa.

Dolphin-watching trips are another popular activity, allowing you to observe these lively creatures in their natural environment. Several kinds of dolphins live in the seas near Gibraltar and are frequently seen. It's an incredible experience to see these elegant animals leap and frolic in the surf.

As the sun sets, the port area becomes more active. Waterfront restaurants and pubs serve a wide range of foods, including fresh seafood and foreign cuisine. Enjoying supper while watching the harbor lights reflect on the sea is the ideal way to conclude the day.

Arriving in Gibraltar by water is more than simply a means of transportation; it is also an experience. The travel, the first view of the Rock, the inviting harbor, and the thriving nautical culture all contribute to an unforgettable introduction to this unique area. Whether you're a history enthusiast, a nature lover, or just searching for a new adventure, Gibraltar by water provides an exciting start to your vacation.

Road and Border Crossings

Traveling to Gibraltar by vehicle and crossing the border is an unforgettable experience, especially considering the territory's tiny size and important location. The trip is much more than just getting to your goal; it's also about seeing the region's unique combination of cultures and landscapes.

The majority of road travelers to Gibraltar arrive from Spain, crossing from the nearby town of La Línea de la Concepción. The border crossing is a fascinating part of the tour, reminding us of Gibraltar's position as a British Overseas Territory. While it's a simple operation for most people, it preserves a sense of historical significance and modern convenience.

When you arrive at the border, you'll see a combination of British and Spanish influences. The signage alternates between English and Spanish, and the atmosphere is a distinctive mix of the two cultures. Whether you're driving, taking the bus, or strolling, border officers will promptly lead you through the essential inspections. Don't forget your passport or ID; these are required for the crossing.

One of the most exciting elements of entering Gibraltar is crossing the airport runway. Yes, you read it correctly. The major road, Winston Churchill Avenue, crosses the runway at

Gibraltar International Airport. When planes land or take off, all traffic, including automotive and pedestrian, comes to a standstill. It's a bizarre feeling to be at the crossroads of road travel and flight, and it's unique to Gibraltar.

The first thing you may notice when crossing into Gibraltar is a difference in atmosphere. The lively streets, famous red telephone booths, and variety of dialects all indicate that you've arrived in a different world. Despite its tiny size, Gibraltar offers a variety of experiences, and traveling by road allows you to take in the views at your speed.

Gibraltar's road system is uncomplicated, with clear signs and well-maintained roadways. Driving here is a pleasurable experience, with breathtaking scenery and convenient access to major sites. Whether you're visiting the Upper Rock Nature Reserve to see the Barbary macaques or seeing the old Moorish Castle, the travel is part of the experience.

The walk from the border to the town center is nice and takes around 20 minutes. Along the route, you'll see important sights and gain a taste of the local culture. The short distance makes it ideal for day trips from Spain, and the pedestrian-friendly paths are a plus for those who like to explore on foot.

Gibraltar's public transit system is efficient and tourist-friendly. Buses operate frequently and link all important sites, making it convenient to travel about without a car. The bus drivers are typically quite friendly, and it's an excellent chance to meet people and learn more about the region.

Whether you're traveling by vehicle, bus, or foot, crossing the Gibraltar border is an unforgettable experience. It serves as a reminder of the territory's unique position at a cultural and historical crossroads. From the minute you cross the runway, you become a part of Gibraltar's fascinating story.

Local Transportation

One of the most convenient methods to get to Gibraltar is via bus. Gibraltar Bus Company operates a local bus service that connects all important locations of interest, including the town center, beaches, and historical monuments. The buses are contemporary, comfortable, and air-conditioned, making them ideal for both short journeys and extended excursions. Tickets may be purchased directly from the driver, and there is also a simple day pass option for those who use the bus regularly. The routes are well-marked, and timetables are widely available at bus stations and online, allowing you to organize your trips with ease.

Taxis are easily accessible and provide a versatile mode of transportation for a more personalized experience. Gibraltar's cab drivers are educated about the area and frequently serve as informal tour guides, providing insights and recommendations for the finest places to visit. Taxis can be hailed on the street, located at authorized taxi stands, or reserved in advance. The costs are affordable, and the service is typically consistent, making it an excellent choice for individuals who like door-to-door service.

If you're feeling brave, hiring a bike is another excellent way to see Gibraltar. Several rental firms provide bikes for riders of all skill levels, and the territory's compact size makes it easy to explore on two wheels. The coastal roads provide picturesque routes with spectacular views of the Mediterranean, and cycling is a pleasant and environmentally beneficial way to explore the area at your leisure. There are also guided bike excursions available if you prefer a more structured experience with local insights.

Walking is possibly the greatest way to experience Gibraltar's charm. The land is small enough to explore on foot, and many of the main attractions are within walking distance of one another. The pedestrian-friendly lanes of the town center are dotted with shops, cafés, and historical buildings, allowing for a pleasant promenade. Walking also helps you to find hidden treasures and lesser-known locations that you might otherwise overlook.

The Gibraltar Cable Car, which takes you to the summit of the Rock, provides a unique panorama. Starting from the base station near the town center, the cable car ascends to the peak, affording stunning views of the surrounding region along the route. At the summit, you may visit the Upper Rock Nature Reserve, meet Barbary macaques, and enjoy panoramic views that span from the Strait of Gibraltar to Africa's coastline.

Getting Around the Area

Because of Gibraltar's small size and diversity of transit alternatives, getting about the island is a pleasure. Whether you're visiting the busy town center, historic attractions, or gorgeous seaside districts, getting about is simple and fun.

The local bus service is one of the most common modes of transportation. The Gibraltar Bus Company provides various routes that connect all of the major attractions and neighborhoods. The buses are contemporary, clean, and quick, making them a convenient option for both residents and visitors. You can purchase tickets directly from the driver or choose a day pass if you intend to make many journeys. The routes are well-marked, and the buses operate regularly, so you'll get to your destination quickly.

For those who want a more personal touch, cabs are easily accessible and provide a flexible mode of transportation. Gibraltar cab drivers are noted for their kindness and local knowledge, frequently imparting fascinating facts about the landmarks you pass. You may hail a taxi on the street, find one at a designated rank, or reserve one in advance. Taxis are an excellent choice if you need door-to-door service or have certain destinations in mind.

If you're looking for some excitement, hiring a bike is a great way to discover Gibraltar. Several rental businesses provide bikes for all skill levels, and the territory's compact size makes it perfect for riding. The coastal roads provide spectacular vistas, and riding allows you to explore at your speed. Whether you're cruising along the seafront or heading up to the Rock, cycling is a pleasant and environmentally beneficial alternative.

Walking is another great way to explore Gibraltar. The region is pedestrian-friendly, with several attractions close together. The town center, in particular, is ideal for a relaxing walk. As you meander through the little alleyways, you'll come across attractive boutiques, cozy cafés, and historical sites at every step. Walking also allows you to discover hidden gems and get a feel for the local culture firsthand.

The Gibraltar Cable Car, which takes you to the summit of the Rock, provides a unique panorama. Starting at the base station near the town center, the cable car ascends to the peak, offering stunning views along the route. Once at the summit, you may tour the Upper Rock Nature Reserve, see the famed Barbary macaques, and take in panoramic views that span from the Strait of Gibraltar to the coast of Africa.

Public transit, taxis, bikes, and walking all provide distinct experiences and benefits, making it simple to select the option that best fits your preferences. Whether you're here for the history, the landscape, or the colorful culture, traveling about Gibraltar is part of the experience. Each method of transportation gives a unique flavor to the voyage, ensuring that every part of this intriguing area is accessible and ready for exploration.

The Rock of Gibraltar

The Great Siege Tunnels

The Great Siege Tunnels are one of Gibraltar's most remarkable sites, demonstrating human ingenuity and the tenacity of those who defended the Rock throughout periods of struggle. Wandering through these tunnels seems like returning to a watershed point in history, with every echo and shadow telling a narrative.

The story of the Great Siege Tunnels starts in 1779, during the Great Siege of Gibraltar. This was a key era, when Spanish and French soldiers besieged Gibraltar for three and a half years, attempting to regain the province from the British. As supplies dropped and the siege went on, Gibraltar's defenders adopted a daring and novel tactic.

To tackle the approaching menace, British engineers launched an ambitious effort to dig out a network of tunnels within the Rock. Their purpose was to build a network of reinforced galleries from which they could fire cannons and enhance their defensive positions. What makes this accomplishment even more impressive is that these tunnels were excavated by hand, using just basic tools and pure resolve.

As you enter the tunnels, the chilly, damp air meets you, in dramatic contrast to the Mediterranean brightness outside. The tunnel walls, rough-hewn and robust, serve as quiet monuments to the warriors' tireless labor here. The small tubes lead into bigger caves known as galleries, which are strategically built to house weaponry and give shooting locations.

St. George's Hall is one of the best-known parts of the Great Siege Tunnels. This expansive gallery was named after King George III and played an important part in Gibraltar's defense. From here, cannons could be shot with deadly accuracy, pouring down on the besieging army underneath. The roar of cannon fire must have resonated through these stone hallways, reminding me of the fierce conflicts waged here.

The tunnel builders' creativity is obvious around every curve. Ventilation shafts were painstakingly constructed to maintain a steady flow of fresh air, and the galleries were strategically placed for optimum defensive benefit. Despite the rudimentary equipment and terrible surroundings, the British soldiers established a powerful garrison beneath the Rock.

Walking through the Great Siege Tunnels, one can almost feel the weight of history bearing down. It's easy to imagine the guys who toiled here feeling a sense of urgency and solidarity, driven by the desire to safeguard their stronghold and their companions' existence. The tunnels are a network of corridors, some leading to observation spots with panoramic views of the bay. These vantage locations were critical for tracking enemy movement and coordinating defenses.

The tunnels are not only historically significant, but they also provide insight into the troops' daily existence. Displays and exhibitions throughout the tunnels include siege artifacts such as tools, uniforms, and personal things. These remnants provide a personal element to the tale, emphasizing the fortitude and inventiveness of those who lived and battled in these cramped quarters.

The Great Siege Tunnels are more than simply relics of the past; they continue to play an important role in Gibraltar's history. During WWII, the tunnels were enlarged and modified to use as an air-raid shelter and command center. This extra layer of history emphasizes the Rock's long-term strategic relevance.

As you emerge from the tunnels, you are rewarded with dazzling sunlight and panoramic views of Gibraltar. The stark contrast between the gloomy, cramped tunnels and the vast environment beyond serves as a poignant reminder of the sacrifices faced by those who defended the Rock.

Visiting the Great Siege Tunnels is more than simply a historical tour; it's an immersive experience that tells stories of bravery, invention, and tenacity. It's a voyage into Gibraltar's past, with each twist and turn of the tunnels revealing a new chapter in the fascinating territory's lasting story.

St. Michael's Cave

St. Michael's Cave is one of Gibraltar's most fascinating natural wonders. Stepping into this tunnel seems like entering a mythical underground realm where nature's craftsmanship reigns supreme.

The cave is located within the Rock of Gibraltar at an elevation of approximately 300 meters above sea level. It's a maze of limestone structures formed by the steady, methodical drip of water over thousands of years. As you walk into the cave, the air is chilly and moist, a welcome contrast to the Mediterranean warmth outside.

Legend has it that St. Michael's Cave was previously thought to be bottomless. This belief was fuelled by the discovery of deep trenches and subterranean corridors that appear to vanish into the Rock. The cave may not be bottomless, but its mystery and attraction are apparent.

The main chamber of the cave, known as Cathedral Cave, is quite stunning. Stalactites hang from the roof like pipes from a huge organ, while stalagmites grow from the floor to form a natural cathedral of stone. The combination of light and shadow in this large expanse creates an unearthly ambiance, which explains why the cave has been utilized as a location for concerts and shows. The acoustics are superb, and hearing music reverberating through the cavern is very beautiful.

Lower St. Michael's Cave is one of the cave's most remarkable features. This bottom part was discovered in 1942, during World War II, and revealed even more of the underground paradise. The discovery of a subterranean lake added to the cave's mystery and made it a focus of continuing investigation and research.

St. Michael's Cave has a fascinating history that goes far beyond its natural beauty. Archaeological evidence suggests that people have utilized the cave for thousands of years. Artifacts from the Neolithic period have been recovered here, showing that the cavern provided early residents of the Rock with refuge and maybe spiritual significance. Later, during Roman times, the cave was thought to be a sanctuary, with old Roman coins discovered within its depths.

During your stay, you'll also come upon a network of well-lit walkways that lead you around the cave's chambers. Informative inscriptions and displays explain the geological processes that formed the cave, as well as the historical significance of this natural wonder. The guided tours are a fantastic opportunity to learn about the cave's various aspects, including its geological origins and the stories and tales that surround it.

In addition to its natural and historical attractions, St. Michael's Cave is home to a distinct animal ecology. Bats, amphibians, and insects have adapted to the cave's environment, increasing its natural richness. While these animals are elusive and frequently concealed in the shadows, knowing they inhabit this region heightens the sense of surprise and discovery.

A visit to St. Michael's Cave is more than simply a geological wonder; it's a trip through history and folklore. Whether you're captivated by its natural beauty, historical importance, or simply the excitement of discovering a subterranean world, the cave provides a riveting experience that will linger with you long after you emerge into the light. It's one of those sites where nature and history collide, resulting in an environment that feels both timeless and alive with stories to be explored.

The Moorish Castle

The Moorish Castle is one of Gibraltar's most iconic landmarks, a castle that has seen centuries of history unfold. Perched high on the Rock, its intimidating appearance evokes the medieval time when the Moors governed the region.

The tale of the Moorish Castle began in the early eighth century, when the Moors, commanded by Tariq ibn Ziyad, arrived on the Iberian Peninsula. Gibraltar, formerly known as Jabal Tariq, or "Mountain of Tariq," was a vital stronghold for the Moors, who constructed the initial fortress to protect their newly acquired land. The castle's strategic location enabled them to control the critical route between the Mediterranean and the Atlantic.

As you approach the castle, the first thing you see is the Tower of Homage, the castle's most conspicuous feature. This huge edifice, with its strong stone walls and tiny windows, was meant to withstand sieges and attacks. The wounds of history are evident on the surface, as evidence of wars waged and defenses held. Climbing to the top of the tower offers panoramic views over Gibraltar, the Bay of Algeciras, and, on clear days, the distant coast of Africa. It's easy to see why this location was chosen as a fortification; the view is unrivaled.

The Tower of Homage's interior reveals its narrative. The halls and passages are a maze of stone and history, with each corner whispering stories from the past. The castle has been restored and enlarged over the ages, combining aspects from many eras and civilizations. The combination of Moorish and medieval buildings provides a distinct ambiance, a fusion of styles that represents Gibraltar's eclectic past.

The castle grounds extend beyond the Tower of Homage and include a defensive structure consisting of walls, towers, and gates. As you go around these sections, you can almost hear the footsteps of the soldiers that formerly patrolled these walls, ever watchful against intruders. The views from the battlements are stunning, providing a bird's-eye perspective of the town and surrounding region.

One of the most fascinating characteristics of the Moorish Castle is its involvement in the different sieges and wars that have formed Gibraltar's history. During the Great Siege of Gibraltar in the late 18th century, the fortress was once again a key point of defense. The British exploited the castle's strategic location to repel Spanish and French assaults and traces of this era may still be found today.

The Moorish Castle is more than simply a historical site; it is an active component of Gibraltar's legacy. Restoration works have retained its structure, allowing tourists to see the castle as it existed centuries ago. Informative inscriptions and guided tours add context and insight, bringing the castle's past to life. Walking inside the castle gives you a feeling of the struggles and successes that have occurred within its walls.

For history buffs, the Moorish Castle is a goldmine of stories waiting to be found. However, even casual tourists will find the castle enthralling. The combination of breathtaking views, rich history, and the sheer presence of old stone walls produces an environment that is both uplifting and thought-provoking.

Visiting the Moorish Castle feels like traveling back in time. It's a voyage through Gibraltar's history, where every stone has a story and every vista tells a narrative. It's a site where history comes to life, allowing you to explore and envision the lives of those who previously lived in this castle.

Apes' Den and Wildlife

Apes' Den is one of the most intriguing places on the Rock of Gibraltar, home to the famed Barbary macaques—Europe's only wild monkey population. Visiting this place is like entering a bustling monkey kingdom, where monkeys walk freely and interact with guests in their natural setting.

The Barbary macaques are Gibraltar's most recognizable inhabitants, and their existence is entrenched in history and lore. Local mythology holds that Gibraltar will stay under British authority as long as the macaques live on the Rock. This mindset has resulted in the macaques being carefully cared for and safeguarded, with their numbers regularly monitored to guarantee their health.

As you approach the Apes' Den, you may hear the macaques' chatter and amusing behaviors before you see them. The den is located in the Upper Rock Nature Reserve, a protected location with breathtaking vistas and a diverse natural environment. The macaques are used to human visits and are typically amiable, yet it is important to remember they are wild creatures. Feeding them is banned to ensure that they eat a healthy, natural diet.

Seeing the macaques in action is a lovely experience. They are extremely sociable creatures, living in groups with intricate behaviors and interactions. You could observe juvenile macaques playing and chasing each other through the trees, adults grooming each other, or a protective mother caring for her baby. Their expressive features and eager eyes give them a striking likeness to humans, which explains why they captivate the hearts of so many people.

Beyond Apes' Den, the Upper Rock Nature Reserve is a wildlife paradise with stunning natural splendor. The reserve is home to several bird species, including peregrine falcons, Barbary partridges, and kestrels. During the migratory seasons, the skies over Gibraltar are alive with flocks of birds flying between Europe and Africa, making it an ideal location for birding.

The reserve's flora is similarly stunning. The Mediterranean environment supports a wide variety of plant life, including aromatic wild herbs and vivid flowers. The reserve's walkways provide many possibilities to explore its floral diversity, with interpretive signs offering insights into the various species seen.

For those who prefer trekking, the reserve has various routes that snake through the steep terrain of the Rock. One of the most popular paths is the Mediterranean Steps, a tough but rewarding walk with breathtaking views of the coastline and the sea beyond. As you go along the route, you're likely to see more local animals, such as rabbits, lizards, and a variety of insects.

Apes' Den and the Upper Rock Nature Reserve provide more than just the opportunity to witness Barbary macaques; they also provide an immersive experience in Gibraltar's natural environment. The combination of animals, breathtaking vistas, and lush vegetation produces a setting that is both wild and inviting. It serves as a reminder of the necessity of protecting these natural areas and the animals that live there.

When you leave the reserve, you bring with you memories of a place where nature and history intersect. The Barbary macaques, with their amusing antics and expressive expressions, make an indelible impact that reflects the ongoing link between people and animals. In Gibraltar, this link is honored and nurtured, making Apes' Den a must-see attraction.

Panoramic Views and Trails

Gibraltar's spectacular terrain and picturesque panoramas provide some of the most breathtaking panoramic views anyone can imagine. The steep terrain and strategic placement of the Rock allow several possibilities to enjoy the beautiful landscape from various vantage points and routes.

The summit of the Rock of Gibraltar is home to one of the most recognizable vistas. On clear days, this location, accessible via cable car, provides a panoramic 360-degree panorama that spans across the Strait of Gibraltar to the Moroccan coast. Standing at the summit, you can see the Mediterranean Sea and the Atlantic Ocean merge into the horizon, with the Spanish coastline to the north and the wide expanse of the African continent to the south. It's a spot where geography and history intersect, giving a sense of the strategic importance of this small but crucial region.

The Mediterranean Steps trek is a must-see for individuals who enjoy hiking and wish to see the beauty of Gibraltar up close. This difficult route makes its way up the eastern face of the Rock, providing breathtaking vistas at each bend. As you trek, you will pass through a varied environment of rocky outcrops, rich greenery, and spectacular cliffs. The steps might be steep and difficult, but the reward at the summit is worth it. From here, one can see the turquoise seas of the Mediterranean, the rough shoreline, and the lush vegetation that clings to the steep slopes.

Europa Point, Gibraltar's southernmost point, is also a great place to get panoramic views. The Europa Point Lighthouse serves as a sentinel, directing ships through the strait. From this vantage point, you can see the Atlantic and Mediterranean colliding, with waves pounding against the rocky beach. The views here are most breathtaking at dawn and sunset when the sky is painted orange and pink and the distant peaks of Morocco's Rif Mountains are silhouetted against the horizon.

The Alameda Gardens in Gibraltar provide a calm respite for a more leisurely walk with spectacular views. These botanical gardens are a beautiful sanctuary, complete with exotic flora, shady paths, and tranquil ponds. As you go through the gardens, you'll come across various vantage locations that provide beautiful views of the town below and the sea beyond. Many types of birds live amid the trees and bushes in the gardens, making it an excellent place to observe them.

One of my favorite paths is the Windsor Suspension Bridge route. This relatively new addition to Gibraltar's network of trails provides an exciting trek across a suspension bridge over a steep valley. The bridge provides excellent views of Gibraltar on one side and the open sea on the other. The walk continues along the cliff edge, offering further breathtaking views and chances to see animals, including the famed Barbary macaques.

Walking around the Upper Rock Nature Reserve, you'll come across several pathways that lead to stunning views. The pathways here are well-marked and vary in complexity, accommodating both casual walkers and experienced hikers. The reserve is not just a wildlife sanctuary, but it also offers some of Gibraltar's greatest vistas. Whether you're gazing out over the town, the harbor, or the open sea, each route provides a distinct view of this breathtaking area.

Gibraltar's panoramic vistas and pathways give more than simply breathtaking scenery; they allow visitors to connect with the area's natural beauty and historical significance. Every stride you take along these routes, every vista you see, contributes to the fabric of experiences that make Gibraltar so remarkable. It's a place where the trip is just as gratifying as the goal, and each route has its narrative to tell.

Notable Places in Gibraltar

The Town Centre

Gibraltar's Town Centre has a dynamic combination of history, culture, and modern facilities, making it a must-see destination for every visitor. As you stroll down Main Street, you'll see a combination of British and Mediterranean elements. This lively strip is dotted with duty-free stores that sell everything from expensive perfume to technology. It's a shopper's paradise, with plenty of one-of-a-kind items to choose from.

One of the most notable landmarks is Gibraltar City Hall. This ancient edifice, located at the western end of John Mackintosh Square, holds the Mayor of Gibraltar's office as well as the Registry of Marriages. Its magnificent design makes it an ideal location for photographs and a better knowledge of Gibraltar's municipal administration.

The Alameda Gardens are an ideal destination for nature lovers. These gardens provide a pleasant respite with their lush vegetation and different plant types. The gardens are free to access and open every day from 9:00 a.m. to 5:00 p.m. They are an excellent spot to relax and enjoy a stroll.

History fans will enjoy the Gibraltar National Museum, which provides a detailed look at the territory's rich history. The museum's exhibits vary from prehistoric artifacts to contemporary displays, offering a comprehensive picture of Gibraltar's history and culture. The museum is open Monday through Saturday from 9:00 a.m. to 5:00 p.m., and Sunday from 10:00 a.m. to 2:00 p. Admission is free, however contributions are encouraged to help maintain the exhibits.

The Gibraltar Cable Car offers a one-of-a-kind view of Gibraltar. This cable car transports you to the summit of the Rock of Gibraltar, providing amazing views over the town, the Bay of Gibraltar, and even the African coast. The cable car works every day from 9:30 a.m. to 7:15 p.m., with the last ride at 7:45 p.m. Tickets cost roughly £15 for adults and £10 for children, and offer a fascinating and picturesque opportunity to explore the area.

No visit to Gibraltar is complete without viewing the famed Barbary Macaques. These unusual primates are Europe's sole wild monkeys and may frequently be seen in the Upper Rock Nature Reserve. The reserve is open every day from 9:00 a.m. to 5:00 p.m., providing an excellent opportunity to watch these interesting species in their natural environment. Remember to respect their space and refrain from feeding them to ensure their well-being.

For a taste of the local scene, visit John Mackintosh Square, commonly known as the Piazza, a bustling primary meeting spot. Surrounded by cafés, restaurants, and stores, it's the ideal place to get a coffee, people-watch, and take in the lively atmosphere. The area is frequently the venue of cultural events and public festivals, which adds to its lively atmosphere.

Gibraltar's Town Centre provides a diverse range of experiences, including shopping, cuisine, history, and nature. Every area has a tale to tell, and every visitor will find something to like. So, tie up your walking shoes and prepare to explore this interesting area of Gibraltar, where the past and present merge to create a memorable journey.

Upper Town

Upper Town, Gibraltar's historical center, is a compelling region that combines old-world elegance with bustling local life. This region, poised on the Rock's slopes, offers a fascinating peek into Gibraltar's history as well as several modern-day attractions.

Upper Town's alleys are small and meandering, with classic residences featuring colorful facades and beautiful balconies. This region is rich in history, and as you walk through its labyrinthine lanes, you'll see several places of interest that illustrate the tale of Gibraltar's growth.

The Moorish Castle is a prominent sight in Upper Town. This majestic stronghold dates back to the eighth century and has stood silently witness to many of the region's historical events. The castle's primary component, the Tower of Homage, stands tall and proud, with panoramic views of the town below and the water beyond. The castle is open every day from 9:00 AM to 6:00 PM, with entrance costing around £4 for adults and £2 for children.

Another must-see attraction is the Gibraltar Garrison Library. This library, established in 1793, includes a large collection of books and records that give a thorough look into Gibraltar's rich past. The library's design is as appealing as its contents, with a lovely façade and an interior that oozes old-world elegance. The library is open Monday through Friday from 9:00 a.m. to 5:00 p.m. Admission is free.

For a taste of local culture, the Gibraltar Botanic Gardens, commonly known as the Alameda Gardens, are a must-see. These gardens, founded in 1816, are a green haven in the center of the city. You may explore a wide range of plant species, many of which are endemic to the Mediterranean region. The gardens are open every day from 9:00 a.m. to 5:00 p.m., and there is no admission cost, making it an ideal location for a leisurely stroll.

Upper Town also boasts the Shrine of Our Lady of Europe. This old shrine has been a pilgrimage site for generations and provides a calm break with its tranquil environment. The shrine is accessible daily, and while there is no admission fee, donations are welcome to help preserve the place.

Upper Town's Fine Arts Gallery is a hidden gem for art enthusiasts. This gallery features works by local artists and frequently holds exhibitions highlighting Gibraltar's thriving arts sector. The gallery is open Monday through Friday, 10:00 AM to 4:00 PM, and admission is free.

As you tour Upper Town, you'll come across a number of local restaurants and cafés. These restaurants provide Gibraltarian cuisine, which is a delicious combination of British, Spanish, and North African flavors. Don't miss out on eating the local specialty, calentita, a chickpea flour pancake that is a mainstay in Gibraltarian families.

Upper Town also has some attractive public spaces where you may relax and take up the local culture. John Mackintosh Square, often known as "The Piazza," is one such location. It's an excellent area to relax and people-watch, surrounded by cafés and stores. This square frequently holds cultural events and public festivals, which add to its vibrant atmosphere.

Upper Town is easily accessible, whether by walking from the Town Centre or by a local bus. The region is well-marked, and the trek itself provides breathtaking views of the Rock and the surrounding countryside.

To summarise, Upper Town is a fascinating mix of history, culture, and local life. From historic sites and beautiful gardens to bustling squares and local cafes, this attractive area has something for everyone. So, tie up your walking shoes and prepare to discover one of Gibraltar's most intriguing regions.

The South District

The South District of Gibraltar is an intriguing destination that combines natural beauty, historical significance, and modern comforts. It's an area of Gibraltar that is sometimes disregarded, yet it contains many hidden beauties worth discovering.

Europa Point is a significant attraction in the South District. This is the southernmost point of Gibraltar, where the Mediterranean Sea meets the Atlantic Ocean. The historic Europa Point Lighthouse, which has guided ships over the Strait of Gibraltar since the nineteenth century, sits here. The lighthouse is still active and provides beautiful views of the Gibraltar and Moroccan shores. Nearby lies the Shrine of Our Lady of Europe, a historic landmark from the 14th century. The shrine is a peaceful spot to meditate and provides an insightful peek into Gibraltar's religious tradition.

For anyone interested in military history, Harding's Battery is a must-see. This reconstructed 19th-century gun battery, located at Europa Point, provides insights into Gibraltar's military history. The battery is available to the public, and visitors may tour the well-preserved facility while taking in panoramic views of the surroundings.

The Gibraltar Botanic Gardens, often known locally as the Alameda Gardens, are located in the South District. These lovely gardens, developed in the early nineteenth century, provide a calm escape with their lush foliage and diverse plant species. The gardens are open every day from 9:00 a.m. to 5:00 p.m., and admission is free. It's ideal for a leisurely stroll, a picnic, or simply relaxing and enjoying the peaceful surroundings.

Another notable attraction is the Gibraltar Rugby Football Union. The rugby grounds are located at Europa Point and provide excellent amenities for players and spectators. The club has a thriving community that holds regular matches and activities. It's a terrific venue to watch a game and learn about local sports culture.

The Rosia Bay region of the South District is rich in naval history. Following the Battle of Trafalgar, Admiral Lord Nelson resupplied his fleet in this little inlet. Today, it's a beautiful place to promenade along the lake, with various plaques and monuments reflecting its historical significance.

The Mediterranean Steps, which begins in the South District, is a hard yet rewarding hiking track. This steep, picturesque trail leads up the eastern face of the Rock of Gibraltar, with stunning vistas at every bend. The walk might be tough, but the views of the Mediterranean Sea and the craggy coastline make the effort worthwhile.

Camp Bay and Little Bay in the South District are great places to unwind by the water. These beaches include crystal-clear seas ideal for swimming, snorkeling, and sunbathing. The facilities are well-maintained and include amenities like cafés, changing rooms, and sunbed rentals, making them perfect for a family day.

The South District also features a variety of eating alternatives that showcase Gibraltar's diverse culinary landscape. From cozy cafés to beachfront eateries serving fresh seafood, there's something for everyone. One famous venue is the Red Lion, a classic tavern near Europa Point famed for its substantial meals and welcoming environment.

Traveling to the South District is simple, whether by car, bus, or foot. The local bus service provides routes that cover all of the area's major attractions, and the roads are well-signposted. The region is also pedestrian-friendly, with several trails and walkways providing picturesque routes for hikers.

The South District of Gibraltar combines natural beauty, historical attractions, and modern comforts. This location provides something for everyone, whether you enjoy history, and wildlife, or simply want to spend a relaxed day by the sea. It's a destination where you can take in breathtaking vistas, learn about Gibraltar's rich history, and enjoy the laid-back charm of the native culture.

Catalan Bay

Catalan Bay, also known as La Caleta, is a lovely fishing resort on the eastern side of the Rock of Gibraltar. This lovely harbor is rich in history and features a vibrant, inviting community as well as breathtaking coastline vistas.

Walking through Catalan Bay, you'll note the colorful cottages and tiny alleyways that give the community its distinct identity. These cottages are the remains of Genoese fishermen who landed here in the 17th and 18th centuries, and whose descendants still dwell in the hamlet today. The region has kept much of its original charm, offering a look into Gibraltar's history.

The bay itself is a popular swimming and sunbathing destination, due to its golden dunes and beautiful seas. It's the ideal spot to unwind and appreciate the natural beauty of the Mediterranean shore. If you enjoy seafood, you're in for a treat. Catalan Bay is well-known for its fresh seafood, and numerous local eateries provide delectable meals cooked with the catch of the day. Dining here allows you to savor the flavors of Gibraltar while admiring the stunning coastline vistas.

The Church of Our Lady of Sorrows is a prominent sight in Catalan Bay. This old church serves as the main focus of the annual September celebration, during which a statue of Our Lady of Sorrows is taken to the shore and blessed by the Bishop of Gibraltar. The festival is a bustling event that draws the community together, enhancing the village's dynamic spirit.

For history buffs, the Gibraltar Gin Distillery provides an unforgettable experience. Located near the bay, this distillery offers tours where you can learn about traditional gin manufacturing processes and try various local spirits. It's a great approach to learning about Gibraltar's cultural history.

Catalan Bay is easily accessible from Gibraltar's main town, with frequent bus services to and from the settlement. Once you've arrived, you may easily explore the region on foot. The friendly locals and laid-back atmosphere make it a great destination to spend the day.

Catalan Bay is more than simply a gorgeous beach; it's a location where history, culture, and natural beauty coexist. This picturesque community provides something for everyone, whether they want to relax by the sea, eat fresh seafood, or learn about local traditions. It's an ideal place to discover Gibraltar's distinct charm and friendliness.

The Marina

The Marina in Gibraltar, also known as Ocean Village, is a sophisticated, bustling hub that seamlessly blends luxury, leisure, and a hint of Mediterranean charm. This marina, located on the Rock's western side, is a popular destination for both locals and tourists, offering a combination of high-end services and breathtaking waterfront vistas.

Ocean Village is a leisure destination as well as a marina for yachts. The marina is surrounded by restaurants, cafés, and stores, resulting in a bustling scene both day and night. As you travel down the coastline, you'll be intrigued by the sight of beautiful boats docked in the harbor, with the enormous Rock of Gibraltar serving as a dramatic background.

Dining at Ocean Village is an adventure unto itself. The marina offers a diverse selection of gastronomic alternatives, from gourmet dining to informal cafes. La Sala Gibraltar is one of the highlight restaurants, with a varied cuisine and a refined atmosphere. It's an excellent place for a nice supper with views of the marina. Bruno's Restaurant and Bar serves wonderful meals in a relaxing environment, making it ideal for a casual supper with friends or family.

If you want to unwind with a drink, The Wine Shop & Tasting Room is an excellent option. This cozy place has an excellent wine selection and a nice environment, making it ideal for a relaxing evening. Dusk Nightclub is the place to go if you appreciate the nightlife. This fashionable club is known for its lively atmosphere and breathtaking views from its rooftop patio.

Ocean Village is more than simply food and drink; it also provides a variety of entertainment alternatives. The Sunborn Gibraltar, a five-star yacht hotel, is docked here and offers luxurious accommodations, a casino, a spa, and a variety of recreational activities. Staying aboard this floating hotel is an unforgettable experience that combines the excitement of the water with the luxury of first-rate service.

The marina houses the Infinity Spa, which provides a variety of therapies aimed at delighting and refreshing. After a day of seeing Gibraltar, a trip to the spa is the ideal way to unwind and refresh.

If shopping is on your plan, the marina features various boutique businesses that sell anything from fashion to souvenirs. The attractive environment of these stores allows for a pleasant shopping experience.

Ocean Village also hosts a variety of events throughout the year, including live music concerts, festivals, and cultural festivities. The marina's broad areas and lovely surroundings make it a perfect location for various activities, which contribute to the lively community vibe.

For those traveling with children, Marina Bay Square has family-friendly activities such as a playground and various kid-friendly eating alternatives. It's an excellent spot to spend a relaxed afternoon with your family.

Ocean Village's parking is convenient, with plenty of places for both tourists and residents. The marina is also easily accessible by public transit, with bus lines linking it to the rest of Gibraltar.

Ocean Village Marina combines luxury, leisure, and lifestyle, making it a must-see destination in Gibraltar. Whether you're looking for a gourmet lunch, a shopping spree, or just to soak up the dynamic environment, the marina has something for everyone. Its breathtaking waterfront views, along with first-rate amenities, make an ideal environment for both leisure and enjoyment.

Rosia Bay

Rosia Bay is one of Gibraltar's most historically significant and picturesque spots. Located on the western side of the Rock, this small bay has a rich naval history and offers a tranquil retreat from the bustling town center.

Rosia Bay played a crucial role in the aftermath of the famous Battle of Trafalgar in 1805. Admiral Lord Nelson's fleet was resupplied here following the battle, and it's said that Nelson's body was brought to Rosia Bay before being transported back to England. This historical significance adds a layer of intrigue to the bay, making it a must-visit for history enthusiasts.

One of the key landmarks in Rosia Bay is the 100-ton Gun. This massive artillery piece, installed in the late 19th century, was part of Gibraltar's coastal defenses. The gun is a fascinating relic of military engineering and offers a glimpse into the strategic importance of Gibraltar throughout history. It's located just a short walk from the bay, and visitors can explore the site for free.

The bay itself is a lovely place for a stroll or a peaceful afternoon by the water. The clear, shallow waters make it a popular spot for swimming and snorkeling. The small, pebbly beach is perfect for sunbathing, and the surrounding rocks and cliffs provide shelter from the wind, creating a serene environment.

For a bit of adventure, consider exploring the area around Rosia Bay. The rocky coastline is dotted with small coves and tidal pools, perfect for a bit of exploration. You might even spot some local marine life, including crabs, fish, and sea urchins. It's a great spot for families and anyone looking to connect with nature.

Europa Point

Europa Point is Gibraltar's southernmost point, with stunning vistas and a rich history and culture. It is where the Mediterranean Sea meets the Atlantic Ocean, and on a clear day, you can see Africa's coastline in the distance.

Europa Point's most recognizable sight is the Europa Point Lighthouse, a light that has guided ships through the Strait of Gibraltar since 1841. The lighthouse, which is still active today, stands majestically against the backdrop of the sea, and its bright red and white tower provides an excellent photo opportunity. Walking around the lighthouse, one can sense the history and maritime significance that this location possesses.

Nearby lies the Shrine of Our Lady of Europe, a significant pilgrimage destination that has been there for centuries. This calm and tastefully kept shrine, dedicated to the Virgin Mary, provides a peaceful refuge with breathtaking views of the surrounding countryside. It is open every day, and while there is no admission price, donations are encouraged to help preserve the place.

Another attraction of Europa Point is Harding's Battery, a rebuilt 19th-century gun battery that provides insight into Gibraltar's military history. The battery is furnished with informational plaques that explain its history and significance. As you browse the site, you will obtain a better appreciation of Gibraltar's strategic importance over the years.

Europa Point also houses the University of Gibraltar and the Gibraltar National Observatory, both of which are educational and scientific institutions. The observatory provides intriguing insights into the study of the night sky, and while visits must be scheduled ahead of time, they are a one-of-a-kind experience for astronomy fans.

Europa Point is also an ideal destination for wildlife enthusiasts. The panoramic views from the cliffs are breathtaking, and it is not unusual to spot migratory birds, whales, and dolphins in the waters underneath. There are various seats and picnic places where you can rest and enjoy the natural beauty, making it an excellent spot for a relaxing afternoon.

For families, Europa Point Park is an excellent place for youngsters to play and explore. The park features a lighthouse-shaped playground that children particularly like. The vast spaces and pure sea air make it an ideal location for a family trip.

If you want to understand more about Gibraltar's history, the Gibraltar Heritage Trust periodically offers guided tours of Europa Point. These excursions offer detailed historical background and intriguing anecdotes about the area's past. Check the schedule for tour schedules and availability.

For dining alternatives, the adjacent Iberian Bar & Grill has a fantastic assortment of Mediterranean-inspired food. It's a nice area to eat and take in the views of the Strait.

Getting to Europa Point is simple. It's a short drive from the town center, and there are plenty of parking places. If you prefer public transit, local buses operate often to Europa Point, making it accessible even if you do not own a car.

Europa Point is one of Gibraltar's most picturesque and historically significant places. Whether you're here for the breathtaking vistas, and historical sites, or simply to spend a tranquil afternoon by the sea, Europa Point provides a wonderful experience that reflects the spirit of Gibraltar's distinct beauty and strategic importance.

Queensway Quay Marina

Queensway Quay Marina is one of Gibraltar's top locations for luxury boats and sailors, combining contemporary conveniences with picturesque beauty. The marina, located at the entry to the Mediterranean, is a popular destination for both residents and foreign visitors seeking to experience Gibraltar's marine appeal.

When you enter Queensway Quay Marina, you'll note the beautiful boats anchored along the spotless docks. The marina has excellent amenities, including 156 spaces that can accommodate yachts up to 100 meters in length. With up to 500-amp power supply and in-berth grey/black water disposal, the marina can accommodate even the most opulent yachts.

A trip around the shore shows several dining and retail possibilities. Restaurants such as The Waterfront and Rendezvous Chargrill serve wonderful meals with breathtaking views of the marina, making them ideal for a leisurely lunch or a romantic supper. The restaurants here provide a variety of cuisines, so there's something for everyone's taste. After dinner, stroll through the marina's boutique stores, which sell everything from nautical gear to one-of-a-kind souvenirs.

For those interested in Gibraltar's naval history, the marina is adjacent to historical locations like Rosia Bay, which played an important role following the Battle of Trafalgar. Exploring this region provides a fuller understanding of Gibraltar's rich maritime legacy.

Queensway Quay Marina also emphasizes security and convenience. Yacht owners may rest easy knowing that the marina has 24-hour CCTV surveillance and a gate-coded security system in place. There are also 24-hour bathrooms and showers, gasoline stations, laundry facilities, and boat lift services. These attributes make it an excellent choice for both short-term trips and long-term berthing.

Gibraltar's tax-free status adds to the attractiveness of Queensway Quay Marina. Refueling is less expensive here than in many other Mediterranean ports, and duty-free shops provide excellent prices on spare parts and accessories. This makes the marina a popular stop for boats traveling to or from the Caribbean or other places.

For those who prefer some leisure and relaxation, the marina offers plenty of options. The gorgeous surroundings, along with the laid-back ambiance, make it the ideal place to unwind. Whether you're taking a stroll along the docks, enjoying a meal at one of the waterfront restaurants, or simply soaking in the views, Queensway Quay Marina offers a serene and luxurious escape.

Parking is easy, with lots of options for both tourists and residents. The marina is also easily accessible by public transit, with bus lines linking it to the rest of Gibraltar. This makes it convenient to visit even if you don't arrive by boat.

Queensway Quay Marina is more than simply a location to dock; it's a destination unto itself. The mix of luxurious amenities, historical significance, and breathtaking vistas distinguishes it as an outstanding Gibraltar site. Whether you're a yacht owner, a history buff, or someone looking to enjoy a beautiful day by the water, Queensway Quay Marina has something to offer everyone. It's a place where you can experience the best of Gibraltar's maritime lifestyle and hospitality.

King's Bastion Leisure Centre

King's Bastion Leisure Centre is a thriving hive of activity in Gibraltar. Originally an 18th-century military castle, it was transformed in 2008 into a cutting-edge recreational center that combines historical value with modern entertainment.

As you enter King's Bastion, you'll notice an astounding assortment of amenities built to accommodate people of all ages. One of the most notable features is the bowling alley. With 14 lanes fitted with electronic scoring systems and bumpers for smaller players, it's ideal for family gatherings or a fun night out with friends. Themed bowling evenings provide a new level of excitement, making each visit unique.

Fitness aficionados will like the well-equipped gym, which features a range of Technogym equipment such as cardio machines, weights, and training vaults. The gym is open year-round, including public holidays, so you may maintain your workout program regardless of the season.

The ice skating rink is one of King's Bastion's most remarkable features. It is open year-round and welcomes skaters of all ages and abilities. The rink also has bizarre ice bumper cars, which give a humorous twist to the conventional skating experience.

Skating classes are given to individuals who want to improve their abilities or experience ice skating for the first time.

For climbing enthusiasts, the Rock Boulder Park offers a tough and entertaining climbing experience. Whether you're a novice or an expert climber, the park has something for everyone, making it an ideal location for practicing and enjoying the sport.

The amusement arcade is a bustling area with more than 60 games. From air hockey and pinball machines to driving games and thrilling simulations, there is plenty to keep guests occupied. A designated Play Zone for younger children ensures that everyone has a good time.

The recreational center houses two theatres where moviegoers may watch the newest blockbusters. The cozy seats and contemporary amenities make it an ideal spot to unwind and watch a movie after a day of activity.

King's Bastion offers a varied range of dining alternatives to suit a variety of preferences. The Bastion Restaurant has both snack and à la carte menus, which include a variety of delectable alternatives. It's an excellent spot to dine in a relaxing setting, with both indoor and outdoor dining. Boyd's Bar, located within the leisure center, is great for unwinding with a drink, offering a variety of beverages and a comfortable atmosphere.

The Boyd's Gatherings Area is a multipurpose venue suitable for organizing special occasions, business gatherings, and celebrations. The events room is ideal for every occasion, from a birthday party to a business conference.

The King's Bastion Leisure Centre is conveniently located at 55 Line Wall Rd Queensway in Gibraltar. It is easily accessible by public transit, making it an ideal location for both locals and visitors. The wide range of activities and amenities provided guarantees that there is something for everyone, making it an ideal destination to spend the day with family or friends.

In conclusion, King's Bastion Leisure Centre expertly blends the historical beauty of an 18th-century fortification with the exhilaration of contemporary leisure activities. Whether you're bowling, ice skating, climbing, playing arcade games, seeing a movie, or simply eating, the center provides a fun and engaging experience for everyone.

Alameda Gardens

Alameda Gardens, formally known as the Gibraltar Botanic Gardens, is a lush oasis in the center of Gibraltar. Established in 1816 by the British Governor, General George Don, these gardens were intended to offer a leisure place for people while also beautifying the town's southern entrance. Today, they provide a retreat for nature enthusiasts and a respite from the hustle and bustle of metropolitan life.

When you enter Alameda Gardens, you are met with a thick canopy of trees and a chorus of bird calls. The gardens have a rich array of plants, including many Mediterranean species. The beautifully manicured trails take you through many themed gardens, each highlighting a particular aspect of the flora and wildlife.

One of Alameda Gardens' attractions is the Dell, a beautifully designed area with water elements such as a gorgeous pond and waterfall. This serene location is ideal for a moment of introspection or a leisurely picnic. The Dell is a favorite with photographers, with several possibilities to capture the natural beauty of the gardens.

Botany enthusiasts should not miss out on visiting the Herb Garden. This portion of the gardens has a diverse collection of aromatic herbs and medicinal plants, creating a sensory experience as you walk through the scented leaves. Informative inscriptions explain the functions and history of the plants on show.

Another prominent attraction is the Rose Garden, which showcases a variety of rose species in full bloom. The vivid colors and subtle smells create a romantic ambiance, making it a favorite among couples and flower aficionados alike.

Alameda Gardens also includes the species Conservation Park, which is an essential aspect of Gibraltar's attempts to maintain and preserve the indigenous species. This little zoo is home to a diverse range of animals, including some endangered species. It's an educational experience for people of all ages, emphasizing the significance of conservation and our part in preserving our planet's biodiversity.

For children, the Children's Garden is a fun and instructive place to explore. This area has interactive displays and play equipment that are intended to engage young minds and build respect for nature. The garden frequently organizes seminars and activities targeted at teaching children about the environment.

The grounds also house the Alameda Open Air Theatre, a picturesque site that accommodates a variety of cultural events, including concerts, theatrical plays, and community meetings. The gorgeous background and natural acoustics make it a one-of-a-kind and spectacular venue for live performances.

Alameda Gardens presents a wide range of events and activities all year round. This bright green space is constantly buzzing with activity, from guided tours and educational seminars to seasonal festivities. These events are a great way to learn more about the gardens and engage with the local community.

Alameda Gardens is open every day from 8:00 a.m. to 10:00 p.m., giving you plenty of time to explore at your leisure. Entrance to the gardens is free, however donations are appreciated to aid with continuing maintenance and conservation efforts. If you're driving, there's plenty of parking nearby, and the gardens are also easily accessible by public transportation, with many bus lines stopping nearby.

A visit to Alameda Gardens is a voyage into the heart of nature, providing a calm respite from the metropolitan surroundings. Whether you're a botany aficionado, a nature lover, or simply searching for a peaceful place to rest, these gardens provide a lovely experience that highlights Gibraltar's natural beauty and variety.

Beaches of Gibraltar

Eastern Beach

Eastern Beach in Gibraltar is a pocket of paradise ideal for a day of sun, sea, and sand. This famous site runs along the eastern side of the Rock, providing breathtaking views of the Mediterranean Sea and an appealing stretch of golden beach. It's Gibraltar's longest sandy beach, making it popular with both locals and visitors.

When you arrive at Eastern Beach, the first thing you notice is the crystal-clear sea softly lapping against the beach. The beach is well-kept, and the smooth sand is great for relaxing, making sandcastles, or simply strolling along the shoreline. The moderate slope into the water is ideal for swimming, particularly for families with small children. The calm, pleasant waves of the Mediterranean are attractive and offer a welcome respite from the heat.

One of the most appealing aspects of Eastern Beach is its accessibility. It's only a short distance from the town center, and there are frequent buses that make getting there easy. If you are driving, there is parking accessible nearby. The beach has bathrooms and showers, so you'll have all you need for a relaxing day.

For those who prefer seaside eating, Eastern Beach boasts various cafés and restaurants that serve wonderful meals with a view of the sea. Chiringuito Beach Bar is a popular destination noted for its excellent seafood and laid-back vibe. It's a terrific area to get a bite to eat or relax with a refreshing drink while soaking up the sun.

Eastern Beach offers a variety of activities for water sports lovers. Everyone may enjoy activities such as jet skiing, paddleboarding, and windsurfing. The beach is also ideal for snorkeling since the pristine waters allow good visibility for exploring the undersea world.

Eastern Beach offers more than simply leisure and water activities; it also hosts a variety of local events and festivals. The annual National Day celebrations in September frequently spill onto the beach, resulting in a joyful environment complete with music, food vendors, and lots of entertainment. If you want to immerse yourself in the rich local culture, now is the time to go.

Eastern Beach prioritizes safety, with lifeguards on duty throughout peak season to ensure that everyone enjoys the ocean safely. The beach is family-friendly, with lots of room for kids to play and explore. There are also covered sections to give refuge from the sun, making it a pleasant destination for people of all ages.

For those who prefer a more peaceful atmosphere, visiting Eastern Beach in the early morning or late afternoon may be extremely gratifying. During certain times, the beach is less busy, enabling you to take in the quiet beauty of the Mediterranean in a more relaxed environment.

Eastern Beach is an ideal combination of natural beauty, recreational activities, and local character. Whether you want to relax on the sand, participate in water sports, or have lunch with a view, this beach provides something for everyone. It's a must-see place in Gibraltar, providing a classic Mediterranean experience that will leave guests with lasting impressions.

Catalan Bay

Catalan Bay, also known as La Caleta, is a charming fishing village on the eastern side of the Rock of Gibraltar. With its vibrant history and picturesque setting, it's a beloved spot for both locals and tourists looking for a quieter, more traditional seaside experience.

As you approach Catalan Bay, you're greeted by a tapestry of colorful houses that seem to cascade down to the water's edge. These homes belong to families who have lived in the village for generations, many of whom are descendants of the Genoese fishermen who settled here in the 17th and 18th centuries. This deep-rooted history gives the village a unique charm and sense of community.

The beach at Catalan Bay is a beautiful stretch of golden sand, perfect for a relaxing day by the sea. The clear, shallow waters are ideal for swimming and paddling, making it a favorite spot for families. The beach is well-maintained, and you'll often see local fishermen tending to their boats, adding to the authentic maritime atmosphere.

One of the standout features of Catalan Bay is its seafood restaurants. The village is famous for its fresh catches, and the local eateries serve up delicious, mouth-watering dishes. **Nunos Italian Restaurant** at The Caleta Hotel offers a fantastic dining experience with beautiful views over the bay. It's a great place to try some freshly caught fish or traditional Italian fare while enjoying the sea breeze.

The Church of Our Lady of Sorrows is another key landmark in the village. This historic church is a focal point for the local community and plays a central role during the annual festival in September. During this festival, a statue of Our Lady of

Sorrows is carried in a procession to the beach, where the Bishop of Gibraltar blesses the sea. It's a lively and heartfelt celebration that brings together the entire community and offers a glimpse into the village's cultural heritage.

Catalan Bay isn't just about the beach and dining; it's also a fantastic spot for outdoor activities. The bay's calm waters are perfect for paddleboarding and kayaking, offering a different perspective of Gibraltar's coastline. Snorkeling is also popular here, with the clear waters providing excellent visibility to explore the underwater world.

For those interested in exploring beyond the beach, a short walk will take you to the eastern face of the Rock, offering stunning views and a peaceful retreat from the busier parts of Gibraltar. The walkways and trails in this area are less frequented, providing a more serene experience for nature lovers.

The village is easily accessible from Gibraltar's main town center, with regular buses making the trip convenient. There's also parking available nearby if you're driving. The laid-back vibe of Catalan Bay, combined with its rich history and scenic beauty, makes it a perfect spot for a day trip or a relaxing afternoon.

Catalan Bay offers a delightful escape from the hustle and bustle of Gibraltar's more touristy areas. Whether you're there to bask in the sun, enjoy fresh seafood, or immerse yourself in the local culture, the village provides a warm and welcoming atmosphere that captures the essence of traditional coastal life. It's a place where history and community spirit come together, creating an unforgettable experience for all who visit.

Sandy Bay

Sandy Bay, located on the eastern side of Gibraltar, is a hidden gem that offers a perfect blend of relaxation and natural beauty. This small but charming beach is a favorite among locals and visitors looking for a quieter spot to enjoy the Mediterranean Sea.

The first thing you'll notice about Sandy Bay is its pristine, golden sand. The beach has been meticulously maintained, and the clear, shallow waters make it ideal for swimming and paddling. The bay is sheltered by imposing cliffs, which provide a stunning backdrop and a sense of seclusion, making it feel like a private retreat.

Sandy Bay underwent significant restoration in recent years, including the addition of artificial reefs to protect the shoreline and enhance marine life. This has made the beach not only more beautiful but also an excellent spot for snorkeling. The reefs create a diverse underwater environment where you can observe a variety of marine species in their natural habitat.

If you're looking to spend a full day at the beach, Sandy Bay is well-equipped with facilities to make your visit comfortable. There are restrooms, showers, and changing rooms available, ensuring you have everything you need for a relaxing day by the sea. The beach also features sunbeds and umbrellas for rent, perfect for lounging in the sun or finding some shade.

For dining options, there are a few cafes and restaurants nearby where you can grab a bite to eat. **The Beach Bar** offers a range of snacks and refreshments, and its laid-back atmosphere makes it a great place to relax with a drink. Whether you're in the mood for a light lunch or just want to enjoy a cold beverage by the water, you'll find what you need close at hand.

Sandy Bay is also a wonderful spot for families. The calm waters are safe for children, and the beach's compact size makes it easy to keep an eye on little ones as they play. The gentle slope of the beach into the water provides a perfect area for kids to splash around and build sandcastles.

For those who prefer a bit of activity, the beach offers water sports such as paddleboarding and kayaking. These activities provide a fun way to explore the bay and take in the stunning coastal views from a different perspective.

Getting to Sandy Bay is straightforward. It's just a short drive from Gibraltar's main town center, and there is parking available nearby. Public transport options are also convenient, with regular bus services running to the beach.

One of the best times to visit Sandy Bay is in the early morning or late afternoon. These times offer a more serene experience, with fewer crowds and the opportunity to enjoy the natural beauty of the bay in peace. Watching the sunrise or sunset over the Mediterranean from Sandy Bay is a particularly memorable experience.

Sandy Bay may not be as well-known as some of Gibraltar's other beaches, but its tranquil atmosphere and beautiful setting make it a must-visit. Whether you're looking to relax on the sand, explore the underwater world, or simply enjoy a day by the sea, Sandy Bay offers a delightful escape from the hustle and bustle of everyday life. It's a place where you can truly unwind and soak in the natural beauty of Gibraltar's coastline.

Western Beach

Western Beach, situated on Gibraltar's western coast near the airport runway, is a hidden gem that offers a unique beach experience. This charming beach is known for its soft sands, clear waters, and relaxed atmosphere, making it an ideal spot for a day of sun and sea.

As you arrive at Western Beach, you'll be greeted by the sight of the Gibraltar-Spanish border to the north and the dramatic backdrop of the Rock of Gibraltar to the south. The beach's location gives it a distinctive feel, with planes occasionally taking off and landing nearby, adding a touch of excitement to the serene setting.

The sand at Western Beach is fine and golden, perfect for lounging or building sandcastles. The waters here are generally calm and warm, making it an excellent spot for swimming and paddling. It's a family-friendly beach with shallow areas that are safe for children to play in.

One of the best aspects of Western Beach is its accessibility. It's just a short walk from Gibraltar's main town center, and there are ample parking spaces nearby for those driving. Public transport options are also convenient, with buses running regularly to the area.

Facilities at Western Beach are well-maintained, ensuring a comfortable visit. You'll find restrooms, showers, and changing rooms available, as well as sunbeds and umbrellas for rent. These amenities make it easy to spend the whole day enjoying the beach without any hassle.

If you get hungry, there are several dining options close by. Beachside cafes and kiosks offer a range of snacks and refreshments, perfect for a quick bite between swims. For a more substantial meal, you can head to one of the nearby restaurants in the town center, which offer a variety of cuisines to suit all tastes.

Water sports are a popular activity at Western Beach. From paddleboarding to windsurfing, there's something for everyone. The calm waters make it an ideal spot for beginners to try out these activities, while more experienced enthusiasts will also find plenty to enjoy.

For those interested in marine life, Western Beach is a great place to snorkel. The clear waters provide excellent visibility, allowing you to explore the underwater world and spot a variety of fish and other sea creatures.

Western Beach is also a wonderful spot to watch the sunset. As the sun dips below the horizon, the sky is painted with hues of orange, pink, and purple, creating a breathtaking view that adds a magical end to your day at the beach.

If you're looking for a quieter time to visit, early mornings or late afternoons are perfect. The beach is less crowded during these times, offering a more peaceful and intimate experience.

Western Beach combines the beauty of Gibraltar's coastline with the convenience of easy access and excellent facilities. Whether you're there to swim, sunbathe, enjoy water sports, or simply relax, this beach has something to offer everyone. It's a perfect spot to unwind and soak up the Mediterranean sun, making it a must-visit during your time in Gibraltar.

Camp Bay

Camp Bay, located on Gibraltar's rugged southwestern coast, is a delightful seaside spot that offers a blend of natural beauty, recreational activities, and historical charm. This small beach, known for its rocky shoreline and crystal-clear waters, provides a unique and picturesque setting for a day by the sea.

As you arrive at Camp Bay, you'll immediately notice the dramatic cliffs and the serene expanse of the Mediterranean Sea. The rocky terrain here gives the beach a distinctive character, and the clear, inviting waters make it an excellent spot for swimming and snorkeling. The bay's natural beauty is complemented by the well-maintained facilities that cater to visitors.

One of the standout features of Camp Bay is the **lido complex**, which includes a seawater swimming pool, a children's pool, and a paddling pool. These facilities are perfect for families, offering safe and enjoyable swimming options for visitors of all ages. The pools are open daily from 10:00 AM to 7:00 PM during the summer months, and entry is free.

For those interested in marine life, Camp Bay is a fantastic spot for snorkeling. The rocky seabed and clear waters provide excellent visibility, allowing you to explore the underwater world and discover a variety of fish and other marine creatures. It's a popular activity here, and the bay's calm waters make it suitable for snorkelers of all skill levels.

If you're looking for a bit of adventure, the rocky cliffs around Camp Bay are great for a bit of light climbing and exploration. The area offers several vantage points with stunning views of the sea and the surrounding coastline. It's a wonderful way to appreciate the natural beauty of Gibraltar from a different perspective.

For dining options, **Seawave Restaurant** is a popular choice located right by the beach. It offers a range of delicious dishes, with an emphasis on fresh seafood. The relaxed atmosphere and outdoor seating make it a great place to enjoy a meal while taking in the views of the bay. There are also several kiosks and cafes nearby where you can grab a snack or a refreshing drink.

Camp Bay also has a rich history. The nearby **Victorian Fortifications**, including the iconic 100-ton gun, add a historical dimension to your visit. These fortifications are a testament to Gibraltar's strategic importance and provide an interesting glimpse into the past. Exploring these sites is free, and they are open to the public year-round.

For those traveling with children, the beach offers a playground area where kids can have fun while staying safe. The beach's compact size and well-defined boundaries make it easy to keep an eye on little ones as they play and explore.

Parking at Camp Bay is convenient, with ample spaces available close to the beach. The area is also accessible by public transport, with regular bus services connecting it to other parts of Gibraltar. This makes it easy to visit Camp Bay even if you don't have a car.

Visiting Camp Bay in the late afternoon or early evening can be particularly rewarding. The setting sun casts a golden glow over the cliffs and the sea, creating a magical atmosphere that's perfect for a relaxing end to your day.

Camp Bay offers a unique blend of natural beauty, recreational facilities, and historical interest. Whether you're there to swim, snorkel, explore the rocky cliffs, or simply relax and enjoy the views, it's a fantastic spot to experience the best of Gibraltar's coastal charm. It's a place where you can unwind, have fun, and create lasting memories by the sea.

Little Bay

Little Bay is a small yet charming beach located on the western side of Gibraltar. It's a cozy spot that's perfect for those seeking a quieter, more relaxed beach experience away from the more crowded areas.

As you approach Little Bay, you'll be struck by its intimate setting. Nestled between rocky cliffs, the beach offers a sheltered cove with calm, clear waters. The pebbly shore and gentle waves create a serene environment that's ideal for swimming and snorkeling. The natural beauty of the area is captivating, with the cliffs providing a dramatic backdrop that adds to the beach's charm.

Despite its size, Little Bay is well-equipped with amenities to ensure a comfortable visit. There are restrooms, showers, and changing facilities available, making it easy to freshen up after a dip in the sea. Sunbeds and umbrellas are also available for rent, providing a bit of comfort and shade on sunny days.

One of the highlights of Little Bay is its excellent snorkeling opportunities. The clear waters and rocky seabed create a thriving underwater habitat that's home to a variety of marine life. It's a fantastic spot for snorkeling, allowing you to explore the underwater world and observe the fish and other sea creatures that call this area home.

For families, Little Bay is a great choice. The calm waters are safe for children, and the beach's compact size makes it easy to keep an eye on little ones as they play. The beach also features a small playground area where kids can have fun while staying safe.

If you get hungry, there are several kiosks and cafes nearby where you can grab a bite to eat. These spots offer a range of snacks and refreshments, perfect for a quick meal or a cold drink while enjoying the beach. For a more substantial meal, you can head to one of the nearby restaurants in the town center, which offer a variety of cuisines to suit all tastes.

Little Bay is easily accessible from Gibraltar's main town center, with regular buses making the trip convenient. There's also parking available nearby if you're driving. The beach's location makes it a perfect spot for a day trip or a relaxing afternoon by the sea.

One of the best times to visit Little Bay is in the early morning or late afternoon. These times offer a more serene experience, with fewer crowds and the opportunity to enjoy the natural beauty of the beach in a more peaceful setting. Watching the sunset over the Mediterranean from Little Bay is a particularly memorable experience.

Little Bay offers a tranquil escape from the hustle and bustle of Gibraltar's busier areas. Whether you're looking to relax on the shore, explore the underwater world, or simply enjoy a day by the sea, this charming beach has something for everyone. It's a hidden gem that provides a perfect setting for a peaceful and enjoyable beach day.

Governor's Beach

Governor's Beach, located on Gibraltar's western coast, is a delightful spot that offers a blend of tranquility, history, and beautiful scenery. It's a small yet charming beach that's perfect for those seeking a peaceful escape by the sea.

As you arrive at Governor's Beach, you'll immediately be drawn to its serene atmosphere. The beach is relatively secluded, providing a quiet retreat away from the busier areas of Gibraltar. The fine sand and clear, calm waters make it an ideal place for swimming and lounging.

One of the unique aspects of Governor's Beach is its proximity to the **Governor's Residence**, the official home of the Governor of Gibraltar. The area is rich in history, and the beach itself has a certain elegance that reflects its prestigious surroundings.

Governor's Beach is also well-maintained, with facilities that ensure a comfortable visit. You'll find restrooms and changing rooms nearby, making it easy to freshen up after a dip in the sea. Sunbeds and umbrellas are available for rent, allowing you to relax in comfort as you enjoy the gentle sound of the waves.

For those interested in exploring the waters, Governor's Beach offers excellent snorkeling opportunities. The clear waters provide great visibility, and the rocky seabed is home to a variety of marine life. Snorkeling here is a rewarding experience, giving you a glimpse into the underwater world just off the shore.

If you get hungry, there are several cafes and restaurants nearby where you can grab a bite to eat. These spots offer a range of snacks and refreshments, perfect for a quick meal or a cold drink while enjoying the beach.

Governor's Beach is easily accessible from Gibraltar's main town center. It's just a short walk or drive, and there's ample parking available nearby. Public transport options are also convenient, with buses running regularly to the area.

Visiting Governor's Beach in the early morning or late afternoon can be especially enjoyable. These times offer a more serene experience, with fewer crowds and the opportunity to enjoy the natural beauty of the beach in a more peaceful setting. Watching the sunset over the Mediterranean from Governor's Beach is a particularly magical experience.

Governor's Beach offers a tranquil escape that combines natural beauty with historical significance. Whether you're looking to swim, snorkel, or simply relax and enjoy the views, this charming beach provides a perfect setting for a relaxing day by the sea. It's a place where you can unwind and soak in the unique charm of Gibraltar's coastline

Europa Point Beach

Europa Point Beach, located at the southernmost tip of Gibraltar, is a scenic spot that offers breathtaking views and a serene beach experience. It's a place where the Mediterranean Sea meets the Atlantic Ocean, and on a clear day, you can even see the coast of Africa across the strait.

As you arrive at Europa Point Beach, the first thing that catches your eye is the stunning vista of the open sea and the iconic red and white Europa Point Lighthouse standing tall against the horizon. The lighthouse, operational since 1841, provides a picturesque backdrop to this tranquil beach.

The beach itself is a mix of pebbles and sand, with clear, blue waters lapping gently at the shore. It's a peaceful spot, perfect for those looking to relax and take in the natural beauty of the area. Swimming here can be refreshing, and the waters are usually calm enough for a leisurely dip.

One of the unique aspects of Europa Point Beach is its historical significance. Close to the beach, you'll find the Shrine of Our Lady of Europe, a place of pilgrimage that dates back to the 14th century. The shrine offers a quiet place for reflection and adds a sense of history and spirituality to the area.

For those interested in marine life, the waters around Europa Point are excellent for snorkeling. The clear visibility allows you to explore the underwater world and observe a variety of marine species. It's a wonderful way to connect with the natural environment.

Facilities at Europa Point Beach are well-maintained, with restrooms and changing rooms available nearby. There's also a small kiosk where you can grab snacks and refreshments, making it easy to spend the whole day enjoying the beach.

If you're up for some exploring, the surrounding area offers plenty of attractions. The Harding's Battery, a restored 19th-century gun battery, provides insights into Gibraltar's military history and offers panoramic views of the sea. The area is also home to the University of Gibraltar and the Gibraltar National Observatory, where you can learn about the local educational and scientific efforts.

Parking is convenient with plenty of spaces available near the beach. The area is also accessible by public transport, with buses running regularly to Europa Point. This makes it easy to visit even if you don't have a car.

One of the best times to visit Europa Point Beach is in the early morning or late afternoon. These times offer a quieter experience, with fewer crowds and the opportunity to enjoy the stunning sunrise or sunset over the Mediterranean. The colors of the sky reflecting on the water create a magical atmosphere that's perfect for a relaxing end to your day.

Europa Point Beach offers a unique blend of natural beauty, historical significance, and tranquility. Whether you're there to swim, snorkel, explore the historical sites, or simply relax and enjoy the views, it's a must-visit spot in Gibraltar. The combination of the stunning scenery and the serene atmosphere makes it a perfect place to unwind and soak in the beauty of Gibraltar's southern coast.

Black Strap Cove

Blackstrap Cove, tucked away on the Mediterranean coast of Gibraltar, is a hidden treasure with a fascinating history and captivating natural scenery. This secluded spot, once a notorious landing site for smuggled whisky, rum, tobacco, and wine, carries the name from the sailing ships that found themselves "blackstrapped" while waiting for favorable winds to navigate the Strait of Gibraltar.

Surrounded by rugged cliffs, the cove offers a tranquil haven with its clear, blue waters. It's the perfect place for a peaceful day by the sea, far from the more crowded tourist spots. The pebbly beach and gentle waves are ideal for swimming and snorkeling, inviting you to explore the underwater world.

Nearby, you'll find historical landmarks such as the Moorish Castle and the Shrine of Our Lady of Europe, adding a layer of historical intrigue to your visit. These sites provide an opportunity to delve into Gibraltar's rich past while soaking in the natural beauty of Blackstrap Cove.

For those seeking relaxation, several nearby cafes and restaurants offer delicious meals with stunning sea views. The area is also easily accessible by public transport, with regular bus services making it convenient to visit even without a car.

Whether you're drawn to history, nature, or simply the allure of a peaceful escape, Blackstrap Cove offers a unique and memorable experience. It's a place to unwind, appreciate the stunning Gibraltar coastline, and perhaps uncover a bit of its mysterious past.

Historical and Cultural Landmarks

The Gibraltar Museum

The Gibraltar Museum is a treasure trove of history and culture, located in the heart of Gibraltar. It's more than just a collection of artifacts—it's a journey through time, offering insights into the rich and varied past of this unique territory.

Housed in a historic building on Bomb House Lane, the museum itself has a story to tell. Originally built in the 18th century as the residence of the Principal Artificer, the building later served various roles before becoming the home of the Gibraltar Museum in 1930. Its architecture reflects the layers of history that Gibraltar is known for.

One of the highlights of the museum is the Great Siege Tunnels exhibit. These tunnels, carved out during the Great Siege of Gibraltar in the late 18th century, are a marvel of military engineering. The exhibit provides a fascinating look at the strategies and hardships faced during the siege, with life-sized figures and detailed dioramas bringing the era to life.

Another must-see is the Moorish Bathhouse, one of the best-preserved examples of its kind in Europe. Dating back to the 14th century, this bathhouse offers a glimpse into the daily life and sophistication of Gibraltar's Moorish period. The intricate architecture and serene atmosphere make it a standout feature of the museum.

The Natural History Gallery is a delight for nature enthusiasts. It showcases the diverse flora and fauna of Gibraltar, from the famous Barbary macaques to the unique plants found on the Rock. The gallery's interactive displays are particularly engaging, making it a hit with visitors of all ages.

For those interested in the prehistoric past, the Neanderthal Gallery is a fascinating stop. Gibraltar is home to some of the earliest known Neanderthal sites, and this exhibit explores the lives of these ancient inhabitants. The collection includes tools, fossils, and reconstructions that offer a window into a world long gone.

The museum also features an impressive collection of artifacts from Gibraltar's varied history, including Roman pottery, Phoenician jewelry, and relics from the British colonial period. Each piece tells a story, weaving together the complex tapestry of Gibraltar's past.

One of the most engaging aspects of the Gibraltar Museum is its focus on the community. The museum regularly hosts events, workshops, and lectures that involve local residents and visitors alike. These activities provide deeper insights into the exhibits and foster a sense of connection with Gibraltar's rich heritage.

The museum is open Monday to Friday from 9:00 AM to 5:00 PM, and on Saturdays from 10:00 AM to 2:00 PM. Admission is affordable, with special rates for children, students, and seniors, making it accessible for everyone.

Located at 18-20 Bomb House Lane, the Gibraltar Museum is easily accessible on foot from the town center. Public transport options are also convenient, with several bus routes passing nearby. For those driving, parking is available in the surrounding area.

Visiting the Gibraltar Museum is not just about looking at exhibits; it's about experiencing the history and culture of Gibraltar in a tangible, engaging way. Whether you're a history buff, a nature lover, or simply curious about the story of this unique territory, the museum offers something for everyone. It's a place where the past comes alive, providing a rich and rewarding experience that stays with you long after you've left.

The Convent and the Governor's Residence

The Convent and the Governor's Residence in Gibraltar are steeped in history and grandeur, offering a fascinating glimpse into the island's past and its governance.

The Convent, originally built in 1531 as a Franciscan friary, has served many roles over the centuries. After the British took control of Gibraltar in 1704, it became the residence of the British governors in 1728. The building has undergone significant renovations, especially after the Great Siege of Gibraltar, and now features a blend of Georgian and Victorian architectural styles. The dining room at The Convent boasts the most extensive display of heraldry in the Commonwealth of Nations.

Adjacent to The Convent is King's Chapel, which was part of the original Franciscan complex. The chapel has been used by the Army, Royal Navy, and Royal Air Force since 1900 and is open to the public for regular Roman Catholic services. The Changing of the Guard ceremony, conducted by soldiers of the Royal Gibraltar Regiment, is a popular event held at the main entrance of The Convent.

The Convent is situated towards the southern end of Main Street, making it easily accessible for visitors. The area around

The Convent is also home to the Governor's Residence, which continues to serve as the official residence of the Governor of Gibraltar.

Visiting The Convent and the Governor's Residence offers a unique opportunity to explore the historical and cultural heritage of Gibraltar. The grandeur of the buildings, combined with their rich history, makes for an enriching experience that connects you to the island's storied past.

The Trafalgar Cemetery

Trafalgar Cemetery, tucked away along Trafalgar Road, offers a solemn slice of Gibraltar's history. Established in 1798, the cemetery was initially known as the Southport Ditch Cemetery. It became the final resting place for many who fell during the Napoleonic Wars and succumbed to yellow fever epidemics in the early 19th century.

Despite its name, only two casualties from the famous Battle of Trafalgar are buried here. However, the cemetery's association with the battle gives it a significant historical resonance. Each year, on Trafalgar Day, which falls on the Sunday closest to the anniversary of the battle, a ceremony is held to honor those who fought.

Wandering through the cemetery, you'll find an array of gravestones, some dating back to the late 18th century. The well-tended flowerbeds and peaceful atmosphere make it a poignant spot for reflection. The gravestones tell stories of those who lived and died in Gibraltar's turbulent past, offering a tangible connection to history.

Visiting Trafalgar Cemetery is a quiet, contemplative experience. It's a place where the past feels close, where the echoes of history linger among the trees and tombstones. Whether you're a history enthusiast or someone seeking a peaceful retreat, the cemetery offers a unique glimpse into Gibraltar's rich heritage.

Art and Cultural Centers

Gibraltar is not just about stunning landscapes and rich history; it's also a vibrant hub for arts and culture. There are several centers where you can immerse yourself in the local creative scene and get a taste of the artistic talent that flourishes here.

One of the key places is the **John Mackintosh Hall**, often considered the cultural heartbeat of Gibraltar. This multi-purpose venue hosts a variety of events, from art exhibitions and theatrical performances to lectures and community activities. Its galleries frequently showcase works by local artists, offering a platform for creative expression. The hall also includes a well-stocked library, making it a great spot for both culture and relaxation.

Another notable spot is the **Fine Arts Gallery** on Casemates Square. This gallery is a focal point for visual arts in Gibraltar, featuring a diverse range of exhibitions throughout the year. It's a wonderful place to explore contemporary art and get a sense of the local artistic landscape. The gallery often hosts events and workshops, providing opportunities for both artists and art lovers to engage and learn.

The **Gibraltar Garrison Library** is another cultural gem. Established in 1793, this library is more than just a collection of books; it's a historical landmark. The beautifully preserved building and its vast collection of volumes make it a perfect place for literature enthusiasts and history buffs alike. The library regularly hosts literary events, talks, and readings, fostering a vibrant literary community.

For performing arts, **Ince's Hall Theatre** is the go-to venue. This historic theatre hosts a wide range of performances, including plays, musicals, and dance shows. It's the oldest theatre in Gibraltar and has a charming old-world ambiance that enhances any performance. The theatre is a cornerstone of Gibraltar's performing arts scene and a must-visit for anyone interested in live entertainment.

The **Gibraltar Cultural Services** also play a pivotal role in promoting arts and culture in the region. They organize numerous events and festivals throughout the year, including the Gibraltar International Drama Festival and the Gibraltar Literary Festival. These events bring together artists, writers, and performers from around the world, creating a dynamic cultural exchange.

Exploring these art and cultural centers offers a deeper understanding of Gibraltar's vibrant cultural fabric. Whether you're admiring contemporary art, diving into historical literature, or enjoying a live performance, these venues provide a rich and varied cultural experience. They highlight the creativity and passion that make Gibraltar a unique and inspiring place.

Shopping and Dining in Gibraltar

Main Street and Casemates Square

Main Street and Casemates Square are the beating heart of Gibraltar, offering a vibrant mix of shopping, dining, and historical attractions. These two areas are essential stops for anyone looking to experience the essence of Gibraltar's lively atmosphere.

Main Street is the central artery of Gibraltar's commercial district, stretching from the iconic Grand Casemates Gates at the north end to the Governor's Residence at the south. As you stroll down Main Street, you'll be captivated by the blend of old and new. Traditional British influences are evident in the architecture and the presence of well-known UK brands, but there's also a distinct Mediterranean flair in the open-air cafes and local shops.

The street is lined with a variety of stores, from high-end boutiques and jewelry shops to souvenir outlets and duty-free retailers. It's a shopper's paradise, offering everything from designer clothing and electronics to unique local crafts. The duty-free status makes it particularly appealing for those looking for a good deal on luxury items.

As you walk along Main Street, you'll encounter several points of interest. The Cathedral of St. Mary the Crowned is a beautiful 15th-century church that's worth a visit. Its peaceful interior and stunning architecture provide a welcome break from the bustling street outside. Further along, you'll find the Gibraltar Museum, where you can dive into the rich history and heritage of the area.

Casemates Square, at the northern end of Main Street, is a lively plaza that serves as the social hub of Gibraltar. Once a military area housing barracks and bombproof casemates, it has been transformed into a bustling public square filled with restaurants, bars, and shops. The square is often the site of events, festivals, and performances, making it a dynamic and exciting place to visit.

At Casemates Square, you'll find a wide range of dining options. Whether you're in the mood for a quick snack or a leisurely meal, there's something to suit every palate. From traditional British pubs and tapas bars to international cuisine, the variety is sure to satisfy. The outdoor terraces are perfect for people-watching and soaking up the lively ambiance.

One of the most notable events held in Casemates Square is Gibraltar National Day on September 10th. The square becomes a sea of red and white as locals gather to celebrate with parades, music, and fireworks. It's a fantastic time to experience the vibrant community spirit and cultural pride of Gibraltar.

Both Main Street and Casemates Square are easily accessible on foot. They're located close to many of Gibraltar's other attractions, making them convenient stops on your exploration of the city. The area is also well-served by public transport, with several bus routes passing nearby.

Main Street and Casemates Square offer a perfect blend of shopping, history, and local culture. Whether you're hunting for a bargain, exploring historical landmarks, or simply enjoying the lively atmosphere, these areas provide a rich and engaging experience that captures the spirit of Gibraltar.

Local Markets and Souvenirs

Gibraltar's local markets and souvenir shops offer a delightful way to experience the culture and take a piece of it home with you. From handcrafted items to unique keepsakes, you'll find a variety of treasures that capture the essence of this fascinating territory.

Main Street is a great starting point for souvenir shopping. As you stroll along this bustling thoroughfare, you'll come across numerous shops offering a wide range of items. Look out for stores selling Gibraltar's famous Duty-Free goods. Perfumes, cosmetics, and electronics are popular buys here, thanks to the lower prices.

For something more unique, head to the local artisans' stalls. Handmade crafts are abundant, with items like pottery, jewelry, and textiles that reflect the local culture and craftsmanship. Keep an eye out for the traditional Gibraltar pottery, which often features intricate designs and vibrant colors.

Casemates Square is another must-visit area. The square is often filled with market stalls, especially during weekends and special events. It's a lively spot where you can browse through various goods, from fresh produce and local delicacies to souvenirs and crafts. The atmosphere here is lively, and it's a great place to enjoy some people-watching while you shop.

One unique souvenir to look for is **Gibraltar Crystal**. Crafted in the Glass Factory at the northern end of Main Street, each piece is hand-blown and individually crafted, ensuring that no two pieces are exactly the same. You can watch the artisans at work and purchase beautiful crystal items, ranging from vases and glassware to decorative pieces.

For food lovers, Gibraltar's local markets offer an array of culinary delights. The market on Fish Market Road is perfect for picking up fresh produce, cheeses, and olives. Don't miss out on the local honey and jams, which make excellent gifts and are a taste of Gibraltar's natural bounty.

One of the most iconic symbols of Gibraltar is the Barbary macaque, and you'll find plenty of macaque-themed souvenirs. From plush toys and T-shirts to decorative items, these playful monkeys are a beloved part of Gibraltar's identity and make for great keepsakes.

Grand Casemates Gates at the northern end of Main Street also often hosts seasonal markets and fairs, where you can find even more unique items. These markets are perfect for finding one-of-a-kind gifts and experiencing the vibrant market culture.

When shopping for souvenirs, it's always a good idea to chat with the local vendors. They often have interesting stories about the items they sell and can provide insights into the best products to buy. Plus, haggling is sometimes expected, so don't be afraid to negotiate for the best price.

Exploring Gibraltar's local markets and souvenir shops is not just about shopping; it's an experience in itself. The vibrant atmosphere, friendly vendors, and unique products make it a memorable part of any visit to Gibraltar. Whether you're looking for a special gift or a memento of your trip, you'll find plenty of options that capture the spirit of this unique destination.

Top Restaurants and Eateries

Gibraltar boasts a diverse culinary scene with top-notch restaurants and eateries catering to every taste. Here are some of the best spots to enjoy a memorable meal:

Aquaterra is a standout for Mediterranean and European cuisine. Located at the marina, it offers stunning views alongside dishes like pork cheek and bao buns. The generous portions make it a great choice for a hearty meal.

Paparazzi Steakhouse is a must-visit for steak lovers. Known for its exceptional beef and beef short ribs, it's a favorite among locals and visitors alike. The ambiance is perfect for a special occasion or just a night out.

Rendezvous Chargrill offers a mix of Mediterranean and barbecue dishes. The lamb shank and seafood linguine are highly recommended, and the cozy atmosphere makes it a great spot for a relaxed dinner.

The Lounge Gastro Bar is ideal for those who enjoy a lively atmosphere with great food. It's known for its fabulous Sunday roast and fun quiz nights, along with a lovely location.

Mamma Mia is Gibraltar's most popular Italian restaurant. With a wood-burning oven, it serves authentic pizzas and pastas that are sure to please any Italian food lover.

Roy's Cod Place is a local favorite for seafood. Their fish and chips are a hit, and the friendly service adds to the charm of this spot.

Bianca's Restaurant is a popular choice for a meal by the water. Located on the quayside, it offers freshly prepared food, a sun terrace, and a gin garden. It's great for breakfast, lunch, or dinner.

Vinopolis Gastrobar is known for its international and Mediterranean dishes. It's a fantastic place to enjoy a glass of wine with your meal and experience a variety of flavors.

Little Bay Indian Tapas Bar & Restaurant offers a mix of Indian and Asian cuisine. Their vegetarian curry is highly praised, making it an excellent choice for those looking for something different.

The Clipper is a British pub with a great selection of European dishes. It's a cozy spot to enjoy a pint and some pub grub.

Gibraltar Cuisine

Gibraltar's culinary scene is a feast for the senses, blending a medley of flavors and traditions from across Europe and North Africa. This tiny enclave on the Mediterranean packs a punch when it comes to food, offering everything from hearty British staples to Mediterranean delights.

At the heart of Gibraltarian cuisine is **calentita**, a savory chickpea pancake that's a local staple. It's the perfect street food, crispy on the outside and soft inside, and you'll often find it served at festivals and markets.

Another popular dish is **panissa**, also made from chickpea flour but cooked differently. It's sliced and fried to golden perfection, making for a snack that's both crunchy and satisfying.

If you're craving pasta, try **rosto**. This dish is a Gibraltarian twist on the Italian classic, featuring penne mixed with beef and vegetables in a rich tomato sauce. It's the kind of comfort food that reminds you of home, even if you're far away.

Fish and chips in Gibraltar often come with a local twist. You might get a side of mushy peas or a homemade tartar sauce that adds an extra kick to the crispy, fried fish.

For something truly unique, **torta de acelgas** offers a savory pie filled with Swiss chard, eggs, and cheese, all wrapped in a flaky pastry. It's a flavorful way to enjoy your greens.

Seafood lovers will appreciate **caldereta de pescado**, a hearty fish stew brimming with fresh local catch, potatoes, and tomatoes, all simmered together with aromatic spices. The stew is a testament to Gibraltar's maritime heritage.

Gibraltar's markets and bakeries are a treasure trove of sweet treats. **Bollo de hornasso**, a sweet bread flavored with anise and sometimes filled with surprises like hard-boiled eggs or raisins, is a festive delight, especially around Easter.

Don't miss **pan dulce**, a sweet bread that's perfect with a cup of tea or coffee. **Quesitos**, small pastries filled with cheese, are another local favorite, offering a bite-sized taste of Gibraltarian goodness.

The influence of Spain is evident in the local love for **tapas**. Small plates of **albóndigas** (meatballs), **gambas al ajillo** (garlic shrimp), and **patatas bravas** (spicy potatoes) are perfect for sharing with friends over a few drinks.

Exploring Gibraltar's food scene is like taking a culinary journey across continents without leaving the Rock. Whether you're diving into a plate of traditional calentita or savoring a slice of torta de acelgas, the flavors of Gibraltar are sure to leave a lasting impression.

Cafes and Nightlife

Gibraltar's cafes and nightlife are as vibrant and diverse as the Rock itself, offering a mix of cozy spots to relax during the day and lively venues to enjoy after the sun goes down. Whether you're looking for a place to sip on a finely brewed coffee or dance the night away, Gibraltar has something to satisfy every taste.

During the day, the cafe scene is buzzing with activity. **Latte & Miele** is a popular choice, known for its artisan coffee and delectable pastries. The atmosphere is relaxed and welcoming, making it a perfect spot to unwind with a book or catch up with friends. Their homemade gelato is a must-try, especially on a warm day.

For a touch of local flavor, **The Kasbar** offers a unique blend of Gibraltar's cultural influences. This bohemian cafe serves a variety of dishes inspired by Mediterranean and Middle Eastern cuisines. It's also a great place for vegetarians and vegans, with plenty of options to choose from. The vibrant decor and eclectic menu make every visit a delight.

El Café is another favorite, located near the bustling Casemates Square. It's the perfect place to enjoy a traditional English breakfast or a light lunch while watching the world go by. Their outdoor seating area is particularly inviting on a sunny day, offering a great vantage point to soak up the lively atmosphere.

When night falls, Gibraltar's nightlife comes alive with an array of bars, pubs, and clubs catering to different vibes. **Rock on the Rock** is a classic pub with a twist, offering live music and a laid-back atmosphere. It's a great spot to enjoy a pint while listening to local bands and musicians. The friendly crowd and relaxed setting make it a popular hangout for both locals and visitors.

For those who prefer cocktails, **The Ivy** is a sophisticated bar that serves expertly crafted drinks in a chic setting. The bartenders are known for their creativity, mixing up both classic and innovative cocktails that are as visually stunning as they are delicious. It's the perfect place to start your night out in style.

Dusk Nightclub is the go-to spot if you're looking to dance the night away. Located at Ocean Village, it offers a vibrant atmosphere with top DJs and a stylish crowd. The club's sleek design and state-of-the-art sound system ensure a memorable night out.

The Hendrix is another standout venue, named after the legendary musician. This rock-themed bar offers a lively atmosphere with great music, themed nights, and an extensive drinks menu. It's a hit with music lovers and those looking for a fun, energetic night out.

For a more laid-back evening, **The Living Room** is a great choice. This lounge bar offers a cozy setting with comfortable seating and a relaxed vibe. It's a perfect place to enjoy a quiet drink or catch up with friends without the hustle and bustle of a nightclub.

Gibraltar's mix of cafes and nightlife venues ensures there's something for everyone. Whether you're in the mood for a quiet coffee, a lively bar, or an all-night dance party, you'll find plenty of options to keep you entertained. The blend of local charm and diverse influences makes Gibraltar a unique and exciting place to explore day and night.

Outdoor Adventures

Rock Climbing and Hiking

Gibraltar is a haven for outdoor enthusiasts, offering a mix of challenging rock climbing routes and scenic hiking trails that showcase the natural beauty of the Rock. Whether you're an experienced climber or a casual hiker, there's something here for everyone.

For rock climbing, the Upper Rock area is the main spot. It's home to several bolted routes with varying difficulty levels, from 5C to 7B+. The limestone cliffs here provide a unique climbing experience, but be cautious of rockfall and always wear a helmet. The Gibraltar Climbing Association offers training sessions and events throughout the year, making it a great place to connect with other climbers and improve your skills.

Hiking in Gibraltar is equally rewarding. The Mediterranean Steps is one of the most popular trails, offering breathtaking views and a challenging climb. This trail takes you from the base of the Rock to the top, passing by historic sites like the Moorish Castle and the Great Siege Tunnels. It's a steep hike, so be prepared for a good workout, but the panoramic views at the end are well worth it.

Another great hike is the Gibraltar Nature Reserve Circular Trail, which takes you through diverse landscapes and offers a chance to spot local wildlife. The trail is moderately challenging and provides a peaceful escape from the hustle and bustle of the town.

For a more leisurely hike, the Windsor Suspension Bridge Loop is a good choice. This trail offers a mix of easy and intermediate sections, with plenty of opportunities to enjoy the stunning coastal views.

Diving and Water Sports

Gibraltar is a fantastic destination for diving and water sports, thanks to its clear waters and diverse marine life. Whether you're a seasoned diver or just starting out, the underwater world around Gibraltar offers plenty to explore.

Diving enthusiasts will find several dive sites around Gibraltar that cater to different levels of experience. One of the most popular spots is the **SS Rosslyn**, a shipwreck lying just off the coast. This site is perfect for advanced divers, offering a fascinating glimpse into maritime history with its well-preserved hull and abundant marine life. Another notable site is **Camp Bay**, where you'll find several smaller wrecks and artificial reefs teeming with fish, octopuses, and other sea creatures.

For those new to diving, there are plenty of dive schools and instructors available. They offer courses ranging from beginner to advanced levels, ensuring you can safely enjoy the underwater wonders. **Dive Charters Gibraltar** and **Ocean Village Diving** are two well-known operators that provide guided dives and training courses.

If scuba diving isn't your thing, Gibraltar also offers excellent snorkeling opportunities. The **Catalan Bay** and **Sandy Bay** areas are great spots to snorkel, with their shallow, clear waters and vibrant marine life. You can easily spend hours floating above the underwater world, spotting colorful fish and interesting rock formations.

Water sports enthusiasts will find plenty to keep them entertained as well. The calm waters around Gibraltar are perfect for kayaking and paddleboarding. Renting a kayak or paddleboard is a great way to explore the coastline, offering a unique perspective of the Rock and its surrounding waters.

For a bit more adrenaline, you can try jet skiing or wakeboarding. The waters around **Eastern Beach** and

Western Beach are popular spots for these activities, offering plenty of space to speed around and enjoy the thrill of the open water.

Sailing is another fantastic way to enjoy Gibraltar's coastal beauty. Several companies offer sailing tours and charters, allowing you to explore the Bay of Gibraltar and even venture into the Strait of Gibraltar. These tours often include opportunities to spot dolphins and other marine life, making for an unforgettable experience.

No matter your preference, Gibraltar's diverse range of diving and water sports activities ensures there's something for everyone. Whether you're exploring shipwrecks, paddling along the coastline, or riding the waves, the waters around Gibraltar offer endless opportunities for adventure and fun.

Dolphin and Whale Watching

Dolphin and whale watching in Gibraltar is a truly unforgettable experience. The waters around the Rock are teeming with marine life, making it one of the best spots in Europe to see these magnificent creatures up close.

Several companies offer guided boat tours, giving you the chance to spot dolphins and sometimes even whales. **Dolphin**

Adventure and **Dolphin Safari** are two of the most popular operators. Their experienced crew members know the best spots to find these playful animals and provide insightful commentary on their behavior and habits.

Gibraltar's bay is home to three species of dolphins: the common dolphin, the striped dolphin, and the bottlenose dolphin. These friendly creatures are known for their acrobatic displays and often come right up to the boats, making for some fantastic photo opportunities.

While dolphin sightings are almost guaranteed, seeing whales is a bit more of a rare treat. However, during certain times of the year, particularly in spring and autumn, you might spot orcas, pilot whales, and even the occasional fin whale or sperm whale migrating through the Strait of Gibraltar.

The boat tours usually last around 1 to 2 hours and offer a comfortable ride with plenty of vantage points to watch the marine life. The best time for dolphin and whale watching is generally in the morning or late afternoon when the sea is calmer.

In addition to the excitement of spotting dolphins and whales, the boat trips also provide stunning views of Gibraltar's coastline and the iconic Rock itself. It's a wonderful way to see the natural beauty of the area from a different perspective.

If you're planning a trip to Gibraltar, booking a dolphin or whale watching tour is a must-do activity. It's a perfect blend of adventure, relaxation, and education, and it's suitable for all ages. Plus, it's an excellent opportunity to connect with nature and witness the incredible marine life that thrives in these waters.

Bird Watching and Nature Reserves

Bird watching in Gibraltar is a fascinating experience, thanks to its unique location at the crossroads of Europe and Africa. The Rock is a crucial stopover for migratory birds, making it a paradise for bird enthusiasts. With its varied habitats and stunning landscapes, Gibraltar offers plenty of opportunities to observe a wide range of bird species.

The **Gibraltar Nature Reserve** is the go-to spot for bird watching. Covering much of the Upper Rock area, the reserve is home to an impressive array of birdlife. During the spring and autumn migrations, you can witness thousands of birds passing through, including species like the black kite, honey buzzard, and booted eagle. The sheer number and diversity of birds make these seasons particularly exciting for bird watchers.

One of the highlights of bird watching in Gibraltar is the chance to see **raptors**. The Rock's cliffs and vantage points provide excellent observation spots for birds of prey. Keep an eye out for species like the peregrine falcon, which nests on the cliffs, and the osprey, which can often be seen fishing in the bay. The views from the top of the Rock also offer a fantastic opportunity to spot seabirds, such as the Cory's shearwater and the Mediterranean gull.

Jews' Gate, located at the southern end of the Nature Reserve, is a well-known bird watching site. It offers a panoramic view of the Strait of Gibraltar, making it a prime location to observe migratory birds as they travel between Europe and Africa. The area is equipped with observation platforms and information boards, helping bird watchers identify the species they see.

Another great spot is **Europa Point**, the southernmost tip of Gibraltar. Here, you can often spot a variety of seabirds, especially during the migration seasons. The views of the sea and the African coast are stunning, adding to the overall experience.

For those interested in a guided experience, the **Gibraltar Ornithological and Natural History Society (GONHS)** offers bird watching tours and educational programs. These tours are led by knowledgeable guides who can provide insights into the behavior and habitats of the birds you encounter.

Beyond the birds, the Nature Reserve is home to other fascinating wildlife and beautiful flora. The combination of diverse ecosystems, from rocky cliffs to woodland areas, makes every visit an adventure. The Barbary macaques, Gibraltar's famous resident monkeys, add an extra layer of interest to your exploration.

Whether you're a seasoned birder or a curious beginner, bird watching in Gibraltar is a rewarding experience. The variety of species, stunning landscapes, and the unique location make it a top destination for nature lovers. So grab your binoculars and camera, and get ready to discover the avian wonders of Gibraltar.

Golf Courses and Parks

Gibraltar might be small, but it offers some delightful parks and nearby golf courses that provide a refreshing escape from the hustle and bustle. If you're looking to immerse yourself in nature or enjoy a round of golf, there are a few key spots you won't want to miss.

The **Gibraltar Nature Reserve** is a gem that covers a significant portion of the Rock. This protected area is perfect for anyone who loves the outdoors. You can wander through various trails, encounter the famous Barbary macaques, and take in panoramic views that stretch out to the sea and beyond. It's not just about the wildlife, though. The lush greenery and natural beauty make it a fantastic place to unwind and appreciate the tranquility.

Adjacent to the nature reserve, you'll find the **Gibraltar Botanic Gardens**, also known as The Alameda. These gardens are a peaceful oasis featuring an impressive collection of plants from around the world. The beautifully landscaped paths lead you through vibrant floral displays and serene shaded areas. It's a great spot for a leisurely stroll, a quiet read, or simply soaking up the beauty of the diverse flora.

For a family-friendly outing, the **Alameda Wildlife Conservation Park** offers an up-close look at various animals, including some endangered species. This small but charming park provides educational experiences about wildlife conservation and is especially popular with children.

If golf is your game, you'll have to venture a bit beyond Gibraltar itself. Just a short drive away in Spain, the **Alcaidesa Links Golf Resort** offers stunning views and a challenging course that runs along the Mediterranean coast. The blend of natural beauty and well-maintained greens makes it a top pick for golf enthusiasts.

Another excellent choice is the **Real Club de Golf Sotogrande**. This prestigious club is one of Spain's most renowned golf courses, known for its impeccable design and lush, green fairways. It's an ideal spot for a luxurious golfing experience, and the nearby amenities add to the overall appeal.

Back in Gibraltar, **Europa Point** offers more than just stunning views. This area includes a picturesque park and lighthouse, perfect for a relaxing day out. The scenic vista of the Strait of Gibraltar and the African coastline is truly breathtaking, making it a favorite spot for both locals and tourists.

While Gibraltar may not have its own golf courses, the blend of beautiful parks and nearby golfing options ensure that both nature lovers and sports enthusiasts can find something to enjoy. Whether you're teeing off by the sea or exploring the diverse landscapes of the Rock, there's no shortage of ways to enjoy the great outdoors in and around Gibraltar.

Family-Friendly Activities

Gibraltar Botanic Gardens

The Gibraltar Botanic Gardens, often known as The Alameda, are a delightful escape from the urban bustle, offering a serene spot to relax and take in the beauty of nature. Located at the foot of the Rock of Gibraltar, these gardens are a haven for both locals and visitors alike.

Originally established in 1816 as a place for soldiers to unwind, the gardens have since evolved into a lush, green sanctuary showcasing a diverse range of plants from all over the world. The Alameda is beautifully landscaped, with winding paths that lead you through vibrant flower beds, shaded groves, and tranquil ponds. It's a great spot to take a leisurely stroll, enjoy a picnic, or simply sit and admire the surroundings.

One of the highlights of the gardens is the **Alameda Wildlife Conservation Park**, nestled within the grounds. This small but charming park is dedicated to the conservation of endangered species and offers visitors the chance to see a variety of animals up close. From playful monkeys to exotic birds, the park provides an educational experience for all ages.

The gardens also feature a lovely **theatre pavilion**, which hosts various events and performances throughout the year. It's an intimate venue that adds a cultural touch to the natural beauty of the surroundings. Whether it's a musical performance or a community event, the pavilion enhances the overall experience of visiting the gardens.

As you wander through the Alameda, you'll notice a wide array of plants, from towering palms and exotic succulents to colorful bougainvillea and fragrant herbs. Each section of the gardens offers something different, creating a tapestry of colors, textures, and scents. The diverse plant life is a testament to the careful planning and dedication that has gone into maintaining these gardens over the years.

One of the most striking features is the **Dragon Tree**, a fascinating and ancient plant that adds a touch of mystique to the gardens. Its gnarled trunk and sprawling branches are a sight to behold, making it a favorite among visitors.

The gardens are not only a place of beauty but also a place of learning. Informative plaques and guided tours provide insights into the various plant species and their origins. It's a wonderful opportunity to deepen your knowledge of botany while enjoying the peaceful ambiance.

Whether you're a nature enthusiast, a photography buff, or simply looking for a quiet place to relax, the Gibraltar Botanic Gardens offer a refreshing retreat. The combination of natural beauty, wildlife, and cultural events makes it a unique and enriching experience.

Gibraltar Cable Car

The Gibraltar Cable Car offers one of the most breathtaking ways to experience the Rock of Gibraltar. Operating since 1966, it provides a scenic and convenient route to the top of the Rock, giving visitors unparalleled views and access to some of Gibraltar's most famous attractions.

Starting from the base station near the southern end of Main Street, the cable car ascends to the top station, located about 412 meters above sea level. The journey itself takes just six minutes, but in that short time, you're treated to panoramic views of Gibraltar, the Mediterranean Sea, the Spanish coastline, and even the distant outline of Africa on a clear day.

As you reach the top station, you're greeted with stunning vistas that stretch out in all directions. The view from the top is truly spectacular, offering a bird's eye perspective of the entire area. It's a great spot for photography, and there are plenty of viewing platforms where you can take your time to soak in the scenery.

The top station also provides access to some of the Upper Rock's key attractions. The **Upper Rock Nature Reserve** is home to the famous Barbary macaques, Europe's only wild monkey population. These charismatic creatures are often seen roaming around the area, and their antics are always a delight to watch. Just remember to keep a safe distance and not to feed them, as they're wild animals.

From the top station, you can explore other nearby attractions, such as the **Skywalk**, a glass-floored observation deck that extends out over the Rock, offering a thrilling perspective straight down to the cliffs below. The nearby **St. Michael's Cave** is another must-visit, with its stunning limestone formations and impressive underground auditorium.

The cable car operates daily, with frequent departures, making it easy to fit into your itinerary. Whether you're a nature lover, a history buff, or just looking for a unique way to see Gibraltar, the cable car offers a memorable and scenic experience that shouldn't be missed.

Parks and Playgrounds

Gibraltar may be a small territory, but it boasts several parks and playgrounds that provide green spaces for relaxation and family fun. Here are a few highlights where you can enjoy some time outdoors:

Commonwealth Park is a beautiful and modern green space located in the heart of Gibraltar. It features expansive lawns, shaded areas, and a lovely lake. The park is a favorite spot for picnics, leisurely walks, and family outings. Kids can enjoy the well-equipped playground, while adults can relax on the benches and take in the peaceful surroundings.

Bishop Fitzgerald Park is another great place to unwind. It has a children's play area with various equipment and plenty of open space for running around. The park also offers beautiful views of the surrounding area, making it a pleasant spot for a leisurely afternoon.

Victoria Stadium Complex isn't just for sports enthusiasts. The complex includes a playground and open spaces where children can play safely. It's a great place for families to spend some quality time outdoors.

The Alameda Gardens (Gibraltar Botanic Gardens) also provide a wonderful setting for a day out. Within the gardens, you'll find the **Alameda Wildlife Conservation Park**, which is perfect for a family visit. Children can learn about various animals and conservation efforts while enjoying the beautiful plant displays and garden paths.

Ocean Village Marina offers a more urban take on outdoor fun. While primarily a marina and shopping area, it has several playgrounds and open spaces where children can play. The waterfront location adds to the charm, making it a great place to enjoy the sea breeze and views.

For a fun family day, **Eastern Beach** and **Catalan Bay** have playgrounds near the sand. The combination of sun, sea, and play areas makes these beaches popular with families. Children can enjoy the playgrounds and then cool off with a splash in the sea.

These parks and playgrounds provide a variety of options for enjoying Gibraltar's outdoor spaces. Whether you're looking for a place to let the kids play, a spot for a picnic, or just somewhere to relax and enjoy nature, Gibraltar's parks have something to offer.

Educational Tours

Gibraltar's educational tours offer a rich blend of history, nature, and culture, making it a fascinating destination for curious minds. Whether you're a student, a history buff, or just someone eager to learn, there's plenty to discover.

Starting with the **Gibraltar Museum**, this place is a treasure trove of artifacts and exhibits that narrate the story of Gibraltar through the ages. From its ancient past to its strategic importance during the wars, the museum provides a comprehensive look at the territory's history. The Great Siege Tunnels exhibit is a highlight, offering insight into the ingenuity and resilience of Gibraltar's defenders during the Great Siege of 1779-1783.

Heading outdoors, the **Upper Rock Nature Reserve** is not only a haven for wildlife but also a fantastic educational experience. Here, you can learn about the diverse flora and fauna, including the famous Barbary macaques. The views from the Rock are breathtaking, and there's plenty of information available on the natural history and geology of the area.

One of the most intriguing sites within the reserve is **St. Michael's Cave**. This impressive limestone cave system has been an important part of Gibraltar's history, used for various purposes over the centuries. Today, it's a major tourist attraction, and its stunning formations are a natural wonder. Educational tours often highlight the geology and legends associated with the caves.

For a more contemporary touch, the **Gibraltar Garrison Library** offers a wealth of information. Established in 1793, the library is a historical gem in itself and provides access to a vast collection of books, maps, and documents. It's a great resource for those interested in military history, literature, and Gibraltar's role in the wider world.

Another engaging spot is the **Dolphin Safari**, where you can learn about marine biology and the various dolphin species that inhabit the Bay of Gibraltar. These tours are educational and fun, offering a chance to see these intelligent creatures in their natural habitat.

On the cultural side, a visit to **The Convent** and **The Governor's Residence** provides a deeper understanding of Gibraltar's colonial past and present. These buildings are steeped in history, and guided tours offer fascinating insights into their architecture, the role of the governor, and the daily workings of the government.

Gibraltar's **Alameda Botanic Gardens** is an excellent place for learning about botany and ecology. The gardens host a wide variety of plant species from around the globe, and there are often educational programs and tours available. The adjacent **Alameda Wildlife Conservation Park** focuses on the conservation of endangered species and is a wonderful place for both kids and adults to learn about wildlife protection.

Taking an educational tour in Gibraltar is more than just sightseeing; it's about immersing yourself in the rich tapestry of its history, culture, and natural beauty. Whether you're exploring ancient caves, watching dolphins play, or diving into the pages of history at a museum or library, Gibraltar offers an enriching experience that stays with you long after your visit.

Practical Information for Travelers

Accomodation

Luxury Accommodation

1. **Sunborn Gibraltar Hotel**
   - **Features**: Seven-deck static cruise ship, infinity swimming pool, spa, gym, restaurant.
   - **Offers**: Stunning island views, luxury amenities.
   - **Estimated Price**: $234.13 per night.
   - **Nearness to Attractions**: Close to Main Street, Governor's Parade, Casemates Square.
   - **Suitability**: Ideal for solo travelers seeking a unique and luxurious experience.
2. **The Rock Hotel**
   - **Features**: Colonial charm, large balconies with views across the Strait to Africa.
   - **Offers**: Elegant rooms, historical significance.
   - **Estimated Price**: $159.89 per night.
   - **Nearness to Attractions**: Located on the west face of Gibraltar.
   - **Suitability**: Suitable for solo travelers who appreciate history and elegance.

Midrange Accommodation

1. **The Eliott Hotel**
   - **Features**: Four-star hotel, comfortable rooms, central location.
   - **Offers**: Proximity to Main Street, modern amenities.
   - **Estimated Price**: $168.27 per night.
   - **Nearness to Attractions**: Close to Main Street, Governor's Parade.
   - **Suitability**: Great for solo travelers looking for comfort and convenience.

2. **E1 Suites & Spa**
   - **Features**: Aparthotel style, gym, spa, sauna, hot tub.
   - **Offers**: Free WiFi, kitchen facilities, close to Eastern Beach.
   - **Estimated Price**: $159.89 per night.
   - **Nearness to Attractions**: 300 meters from Eastern Beach.
   - **Suitability**: Ideal for solo travelers who enjoy self-catering options and wellness facilities.

Budget Accommodation

1. **Brand New Massive Studio - E1 - Self Catering**
    ○ **Features**: Beachfront property, modern and clean, washer/dryer.
    ○ **Offers**: Bus to town center every 15 minutes, self-service.
    ○ **Estimated Price**: $112.09 per night.
    ○ **Nearness to Attractions**: 300 meters from Eastern Beach.
    ○ **Suitability**: Suitable for solo travelers on a budget who prefer self-catering and easy access to town.

2. **Luxury Sunrise Oceanview Apartment**
    ○ **Features**: Access to spa facilities, wellness packages, steam room.
    ○ **Offers**: Sea views, private pool.
    ○ **Estimated Price**: $112.09 per night.
    ○ **Nearness to Attractions**: 16-minute walk from Western Beach.
    ○ **Suitability**: Great for solo travelers who want a budget-friendly ocean view with wellness amenities.

Health and Safety Tips

When traveling to Gibraltar, it's important to keep a few health and safety tips in mind to ensure a smooth and enjoyable trip:

Stay up-to-date with vaccinations by making sure your routine shots are current, including MMR (measles, mumps, rubella), diphtheria-tetanus-pertussis, and your annual flu shot. Consider getting vaccinated for hepatitis A and B, especially if you plan on eating street food or engaging in higher-risk activities.

Even though Gibraltar has high standards for food and water safety, it's still a good idea to drink bottled water and be cautious with street food. Always wash your hands frequently and use hand sanitizer when soap and water aren't available.

Bug bites can spread diseases, so it's wise to use insect repellent, wear long sleeves and pants, and sleep under a mosquito net if you're staying in accommodations without screens, even though Gibraltar is an industrialized country.

When exploring Gibraltar's landscapes, stick to marked trails and avoid wandering off into unfamiliar areas. Always let someone know where you're going and when you plan to return. While the Barbary macaques are a popular attraction, remember they are wild animals and can be unpredictable.

Keep a safe distance, avoid feeding them, and never try to touch or interact with them.

Practice good hygiene by washing your hands regularly, using hand sanitizer, and avoiding close contact with people who are sick. This is especially important in crowded areas like markets and public transportation.

Use reputable taxi services or ride-sharing apps to get around safely. Avoid walking alone at night in unfamiliar areas and always be aware of your surroundings. In case of a medical emergency, dial 999 and ask for an ambulance. It's also a good idea to have travel insurance that covers medical evacuation and treatment.

Currency and Banking

Gibraltar uses the Gibraltar pound (GIP) as its official currency, which is pegged to the British pound sterling at a 1:1 ratio. Both currencies are accepted interchangeably in Gibraltar, making it convenient for visitors, especially those coming from the UK.

Gibraltar boasts a robust banking sector with several prominent banks providing a range of services. Some of these include Gibraltar International Bank Limited, Trusted Novus Bank Limited, and Turicum Private Bank Limited. Opening a bank account here is straightforward, with options available in various currencies such as the Euro and the US dollar. The banking system is known for its stability and is supervised by the Federal Service Commission.

For travelers, it's helpful to know that ATMs are widely available in Gibraltar, dispensing both Gibraltar pounds and British pounds. While credit cards such as Visa, MasterCard, and American Express are commonly accepted, carrying some cash is advisable, especially for smaller establishments. Currency exchange services are available at banks and exchange bureaus, but using ATMs for withdrawals can often give you better exchange rates.

Most banks operate from Monday to Friday, typically from 9 AM to 5 PM, with some branches open on Saturdays. To manage your money effectively while in Gibraltar, remember to notify your bank about your travel plans to avoid any disruptions with your cards. Checking exchange rates before exchanging money can help you get the best value. When using ATMs, select those located in well-lit, secure areas, preferably within banks or shopping centers.

Communication and Internet

Gibraltar has excellent communication and internet services, making it easy for travelers to stay connected. The country code is +350, and the island has a reliable telephony system that includes both fixed-line and mobile services. Making international calls is straightforward, and there are several options to stay in touch with friends and family back home.

When it comes to internet access, Gibraltar doesn't disappoint. With around 94% of residents having internet access and approximately 70% enjoying fast connections, you'll find reliable Wi-Fi in most hotels, hostels, and rental apartments.

Mobile networks in Gibraltar are well-developed, allowing you to use your mobile phone just as you would at home. Several providers offer competitive plans and coverage, so it's a good idea to check with your home provider about international roaming options. Alternatively, consider purchasing a local SIM card for better rates on calls, texts, and data.

For internet access, many cafes, restaurants, and public areas offer free Wi-Fi, so you can stay connected while exploring.

Before traveling, make sure your mobile phone is compatible with Gibraltar's network frequencies and consider getting a local SIM card for better rates. With these communication and internet options, staying connected during your time in Gibraltar will be a breeze. If you have any specific questions or need more details, feel free to ask!

CONCLUSION

We've been on quite the tour through Gibraltar, a dynamic and complex location. Gibraltar has something for everyone, from its rich history and distinct cultural blend to its spectacular natural surroundings and modern facilities.

Exploring the ancient depths of Gibraltar, we discover a story that spans thousands of years. This small but strategically crucial peninsula has been inhabited by a variety of cultures, including Phoenicians, Romans, Moors, and British. The Rock of Gibraltar is a gigantic emblem of perseverance and power, mirroring the innumerable stories of sieges, conflicts, and periods of peace that have molded the country's character.

Our tour through Gibraltar's history takes us to prominent sites such as the Great Siege Tunnels and the Moorish Castle. These places are more than simply historical ruins; they are living museums that provide an insight into the inventiveness and perseverance of people who came before us. Walking through these ancient locations, one can practically hear the echoes of troops, the clanging of swords, and the strategic talks that have left an indelible stamp on Gibraltar's terrain.

But Gibraltar is more than simply its history; it is a dynamic, living creature that is always evolving. The juxtaposition of modernism with this historical setting is stunning. Walking down Main Street, you'll see a mix of British high-street stores, local boutiques, and delightful cafés. The busy Casemates Square, originally a military bastion, is now a hive of activity where residents and tourists mix, dine, and watch live entertainment.

Gibraltar's natural splendor adds another captivating chapter to our adventure. The Upper Rock Nature Reserve is a flora and wildlife refuge where the famed Barbary macaques may walk freely. These mischievous primates, Europe's only wild monkeys, offer a fun element to the area. The panoramic views from the Rock are stunning, with a vantage point that extends over the Strait to Africa. It serves as a reminder of Gibraltar's unique geographic location at the confluence of two continents.

We venture into the depths of St. Michael's Cave, where we discover a subterranean marvel that has captivated and perplexed visitors for ages. The cave's magnificent stalactites and stalagmites create an unearthly atmosphere, which is enhanced by the intriguing mythology and history linked with it. The cave also makes an excellent site for concerts and gatherings, combining natural beauty with cultural activities.

Gibraltar's seas are filled with marine life, making it a diving and snorkeling paradise. Underwater exploration can lead to the discovery of shipwreck remains, beautiful coral reefs, and a variety of aquatic species. Dolphin and whale watching trips provide an amazing experience as you observe these majestic animals in their natural habitats. The sight of dolphins jumping through the waters or the magnificent presence of a whale is a memorable experience.

Rock climbing and trekking on the Upper Rock offer an exciting challenge for adventurers. The Mediterranean Steps, with their steep rise and harsh terrain, provide a spiritual and sensory experience as well as a physical workout. The ascent is rewarded with breathtaking sights and a sense of achievement.

Gibraltar's gastronomic environment reflects the territory's numerous cultural influences. The cuisine here is diverse, ranging from conventional British fare to Mediterranean and North African delicacies. Dining in Gibraltar is an adventure in and of itself, with opportunities to savor freshly caught fish, delectable tapas, and substantial stews. The dynamic culinary scene is supported by a variety of dining alternatives, including fancy restaurants, cozy cafés, and beachfront shacks.

Gibraltar's nighttime is equally diversified as its daytime activities. Whether you like a peaceful evening at a bar, dancing the night away in a fashionable club, or listening to live music, there is something for everyone. The local bars and clubs provide a vibrant atmosphere in which to socialize, relax, and enjoy the friendly hospitality of the Gibraltarians.

Gibraltar's accommodations cater to all types of travelers, from luxury hotels with spectacular vistas and top-notch services to low-cost hostels and midrange hotels that provide comfort and convenience. Because of the territory's tight layout, you'll never be far from the activity.

Gibraltar is a secure and pleasant place for solitary travelers. The friendly inhabitants, effective public transit, and a variety of activities allow you to explore at your leisure and make the most of your vacation. Whether you're roaming around historical landmarks, hiking in the nature reserve, or simply resting on the beach, there's plenty to keep you entertained.

Gibraltar prioritizes health and safety, with state-of-the-art healthcare facilities and a strong focus on sanitation and hygiene. The local authorities are cautious in guaranteeing the safety of both inhabitants and tourists, making it a reassuring place in these uncertain times.

Communication and internet services are great, allowing you to remain in touch with loved ones or businesses while enjoying your vacation. Wi-Fi is widely available, cell networks are stable, and acquiring a local SIM card is simple, making it easy to stay in touch and share your experiences.

Printed in Great Britain
by Amazon

60988873R00090